Non-Verbal Reasoning
3D & Spatial

The 11+
10-Minute Tests

For the CEM (Durham University) test

Book 2

Ages
10-11

Practise • Prepare • Pass
Everything your child needs for 11+ success

How to use this book

This book is made up of 10-minute tests and puzzle pages.
There are answers and detailed explanations in the pull-out section at the back of the book.

10-Minute Tests

* There are 31 tests in this book, each containing 17 or 18 questions.

* Each test is designed to focus on 3D and spatial questions that your child could come across in their 11+ test. They cover a variety of skills and techniques at the right difficulty levels.

* Your child should aim to score at least 15 in each 10-minute test.
  If they score less than this, use their results to work out the areas they need more practice on.

* If your child hasn't managed to finish the test in time, they need to work on increasing their speed, whereas if they have made a lot of mistakes, they need to work more carefully.

* Keep track of your child's scores using the progress chart on the inside back cover of the book.

Puzzle Pages

* There are 10 puzzle pages in this book, which are a great break from test-style questions.
  They encourage children to practise the same skills that they will need in the test, but in a fun way.

Published by CGP

Editors:
Marc Barnard, Alex Fairer, Katherine Faudemer, Sharon Keeley-Holden, Rachel Kordan.

With thanks to Alison Griffin and Glenn Rogers for the proofreading.

Please note that CGP is not associated with CEM or The University of Durham in any way.
This book does not include any official questions and it is not endorsed by CEM or The University of Durham.
CEM, Centre for Evaluation and Monitoring, Durham University and *The University of Durham*
are all trademarks of The University of Durham.

ISBN: 978 1 78294 765 3
Printed by Elanders Ltd, Newcastle upon Tyne
Clipart from Corel®

Based on the classic CGP style created by Richard Parsons.

Contents

Question Type Examples

These pages contain a completed example question for each question type that appears in this book. Have a look through them to familiarise yourself with the question types before you do the tests.

Building Blocks

Work out which set of blocks can be put together to make the 3D figure on the left.

Example:

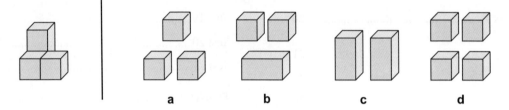

a   b   c   d

Answer: b

The block at the bottom of B rotates to become the block at the back of the figure. The two cubes move to the front.

Complete the Shape

Without rotating the figure on the left, work out which option fits onto it to make the 3D shape in the grey box.

Example:

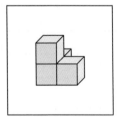 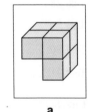 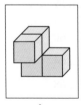 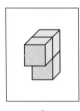 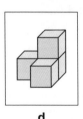

a   b   c   d

Answer: d

D rotates 90 degrees anticlockwise in the plane of the page (see the glossary on page 142) to fit with the figure on the left.

3D Rotation

Work out which 3D figure in the grey box has been rotated to make the new 3D figure.

Example:

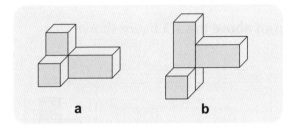
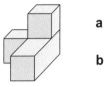

a

b

Answer: a

Figure A has been rotated 90 degrees right-to-left (see the glossary on page 142).

Fold along the Line

Work out which option shows the figure on the left when folded along the dotted line.

Example:

a   **b**   **c**   **d**

Answer: a

The small triangle above the dotted line folds down.

Fold and Punch

A square is folded and then a hole is punched, as shown on the left.
Work out which option shows the square when unfolded.

Example:

a   **b**   **c**   **d**

Answer: c

For the 2D Views of 3D Shapes questions, you could be asked to pick out the view from the **left**, **right**, **back** or from **above** the 3D figure. Make sure you read the question carefully.

2D Views of 3D Shapes

Work out which option is a 2D view from **above** the 3D figure shown.

Example:

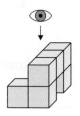 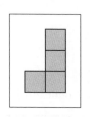 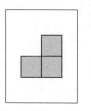 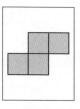 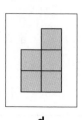

a   b   c   d

Answer: a

There are four blocks visible from above, which rules out B and D.
There is a line of three blocks on the right-hand side of the shape, which rules out C.

Work out which option is a 2D view from the **left** of the 3D figure shown.

Example:

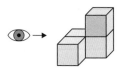 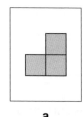 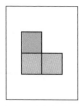 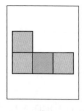 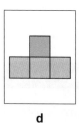

a   b   c   d

Answer: b

There are three blocks visible from the left, which rules out C and D.
There is a blue block at the top of the figure, which rules out A.

For the Different Views of 3D Shapes questions, you could be asked to find the view from the **left**, **right**, **back** or from **above** the 3D figure. Make sure you read the question carefully.

Different Views of 3D Shapes

Work out which option is the 3D figure viewed from the **right**.

Example:

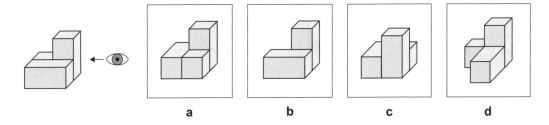

a   b   c   d

Answer: c

There is a vertical block two cubes high visible at the front
when viewed from the right, which rules out A, B and D.

Work out which option is the 3D figure viewed from the **back**.

Example:

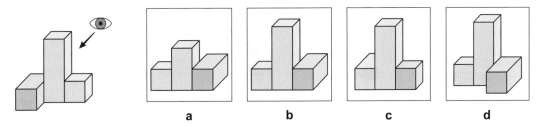

a   b   c   d

Answer: b

In option A, the middle block is the wrong size. The cube is grey, which rules out C.
When viewed from the back, the blue block should go away from you, which rules out D.

For questions involving nets, the net must be folded **into** the page —
see the glossary on page 142.

Cubes and Nets

Work out which of the four cubes can be made from the net.

Example:

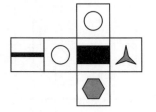

                                      a   **b**   **c**   **d**

Answer: c

There is no black circle, which rules out A. The thick black line and the thin black line
must be on opposite sides, which rules out B. There is only one grey hexagon, which rules out D.

Partial Nets

Work out which of the four partial nets can be folded to make the cube on the left.

Example:

 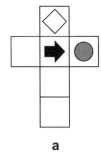 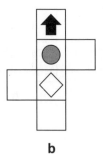 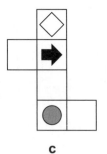 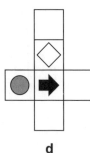

                                    a   **b**   **c**   **d**

Answer: d

The arrow points away from the circle, which rules out A.
None of the shapes can be on opposite sides, which rules out B and C.

Work out which of the 3D shapes can be made from the net.

Example:

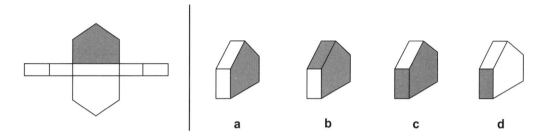

a   b   c   d

Answer: a

In the net, all the rectangular faces are white, which rules out B, C and D.

The figures on the left show different views of the same cube. All the cube faces are different. Work out which of the options should replace the blue cube face.

Example:

               a   b   c   d

Answer: b

In the first two figures, the grey triangle points to the white heart.
So in the third figure, the grey triangle must also point to the white heart.

Question Type Examples

Test 1

You have **10 minutes** to do this test. Circle the letter for each correct answer.

Work out which 3D figure in the grey box has been rotated to make the new 3D figure.

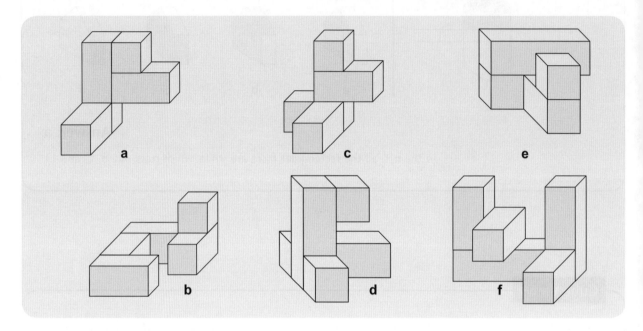

1.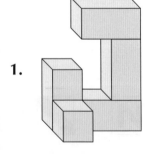

a   d

b   e

c   f

2.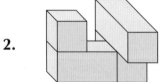

a   d

b   e

c   f

3.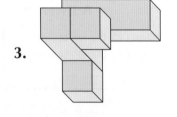

a   d

b   e

c   f

4.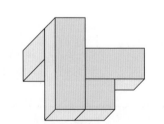

a   d

b   e

c   f

Work out which of the four cubes can be made from the net.

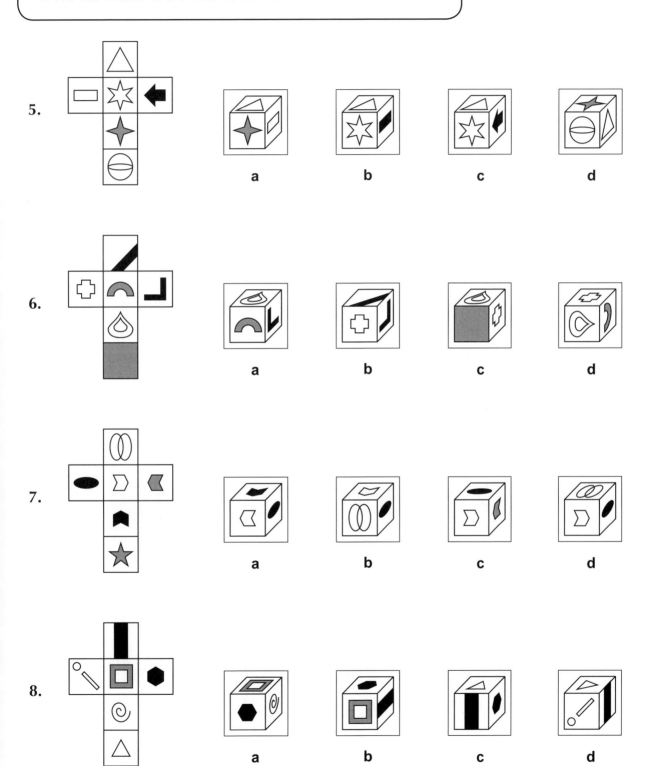

5. a b c d

6. a b c d

7. a b c d

8. a b c d

9

Work out which option is a 2D view from the **left** of the 3D figure shown.

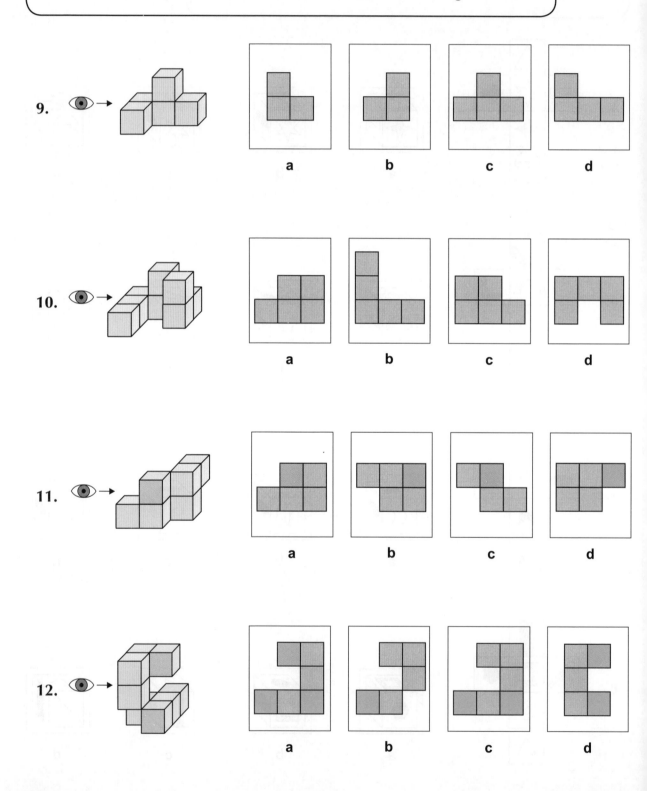

9.

a   b   c   d

10.

a   b   c   d

11.

a   b   c   d

12.

a   b   c   d

A square is folded and then a hole is punched, as shown on the left.
Work out which option shows the square when unfolded.

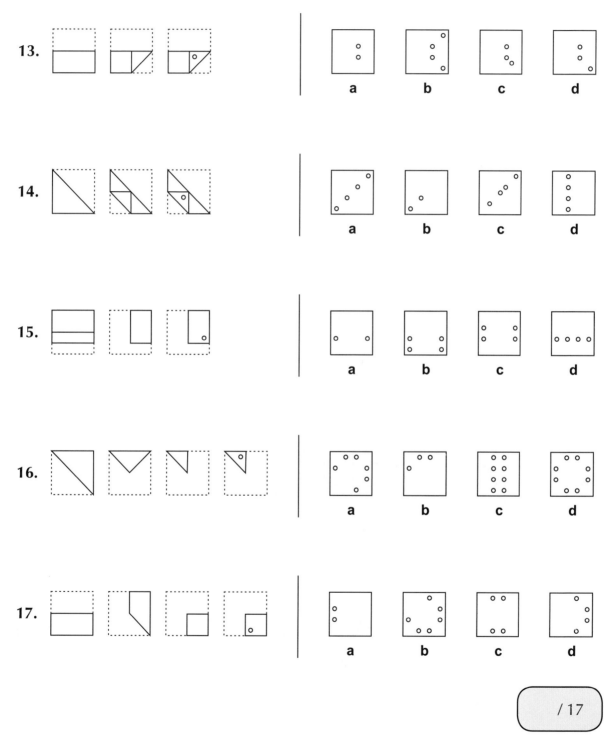

13.

      a   b   c   d

14.

      a   b   c   d

15.

      a   b   c   d

16.

      a   b   c   d

17.

      a   b   c   d

/ 17

Test 1

Test 2

You have **10 minutes** to do this test. Circle the letter for each correct answer.

Work out which option is the 3D figure viewed from **above**.

1.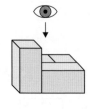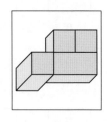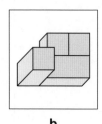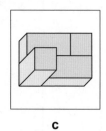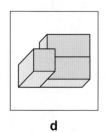

                                          a   b   c   d

2.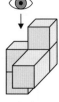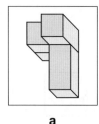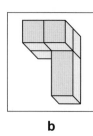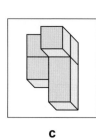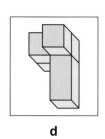

                                            a   b   c   d

3.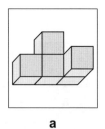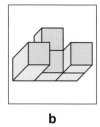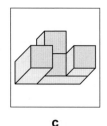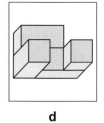

                                            a   b   c   d

4.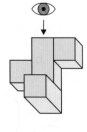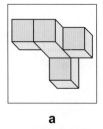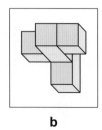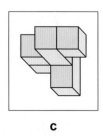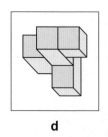

                                            a   b   c   d

                                    12   © CGP — not to be photocopied

Work out which of the four partial nets can be folded to make the cube on the left.

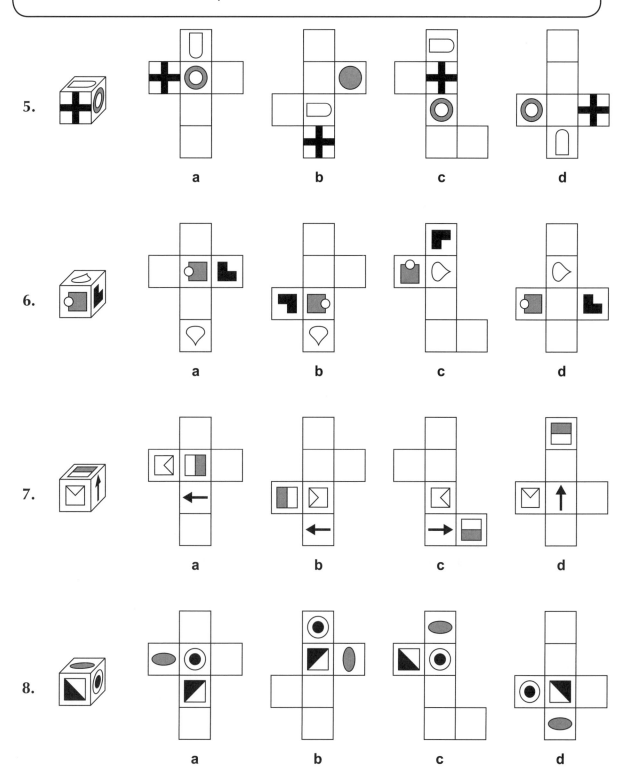

5.

a   b   c   d

6.

a   b   c   d

7.

a   b   c   d

8.

a   b   c   d

13

Test 2

The figures on the left show different views of the same cube. All the cube faces are different. Work out which of the options should replace the blue cube face.

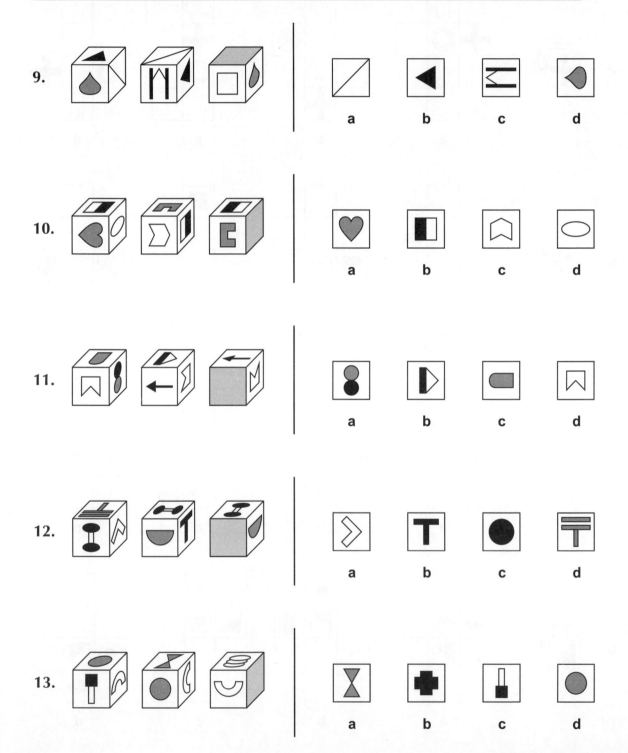

9.

a   b   c   d

10.

a   b   c   d

11.

a   b   c   d

12.

a   b   c   d

13.

a   b   c   d

Work out which option can be put together with the figure on the left to make the 3D shape in the grey box.

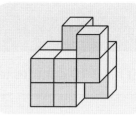

14.

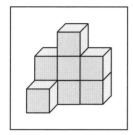 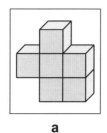 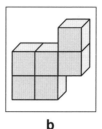 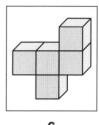 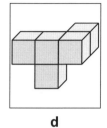

a　　　　　b　　　　　c　　　　　d

15.

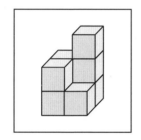 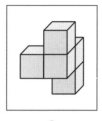 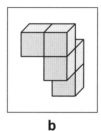 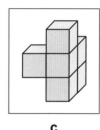 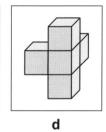

a　　　　　b　　　　　c　　　　　d

16.

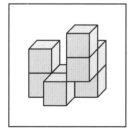 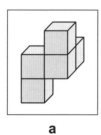 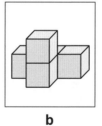 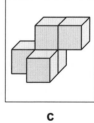 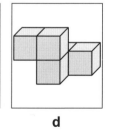

a　　　　　b　　　　　c　　　　　d

17.

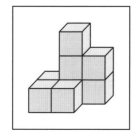 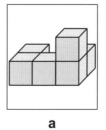 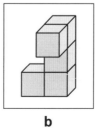 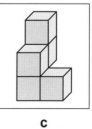 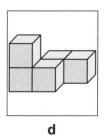

a　　　　　b　　　　　c　　　　　d

/ 17

15

Test 2

You have **10 minutes** to do this test. Circle the letter for each correct answer.

Work out which set of blocks can be put together to make the 3D figure on the left.

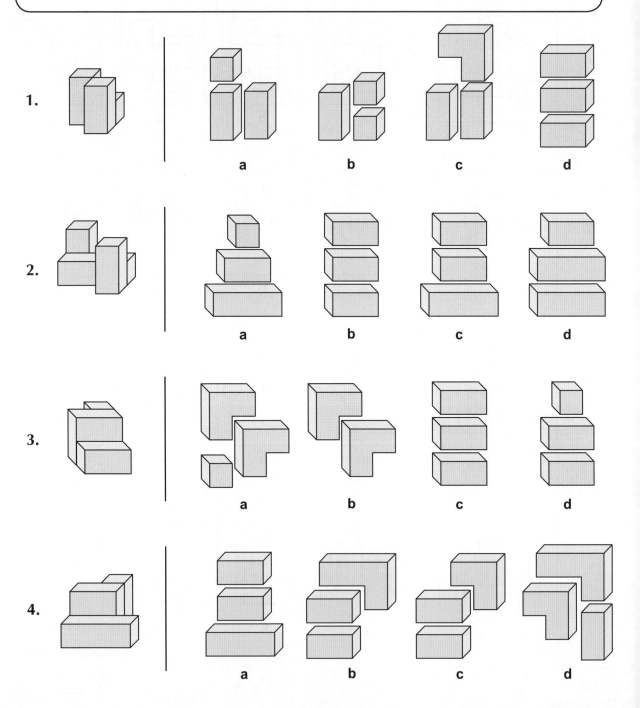

1.

a   b   c   d

2.

a   b   c   d

3.

a   b   c   d

4.

a   b   c   d

16

Work out which 3D figure in the grey box has been rotated to make the new 3D figure.

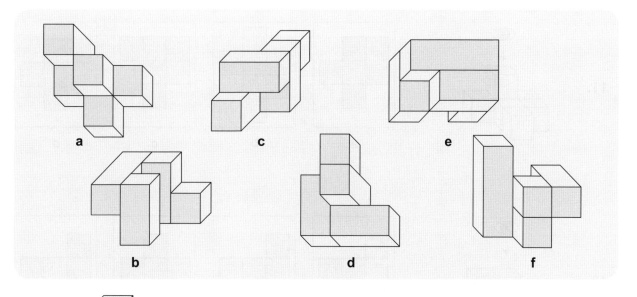

a

c

e

b

d

f

5.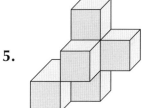

a   d

b   e

c   f

6.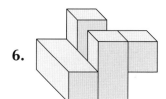

a   d

b   e

c   f

7.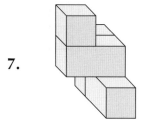

a   d

b   e

c   f

8.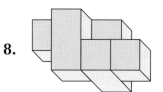

a   d

b   e

c   f

9.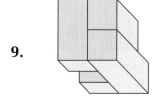

a   d

b   e

c   f

10.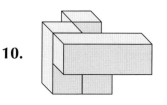

a   d

b   e

c   f

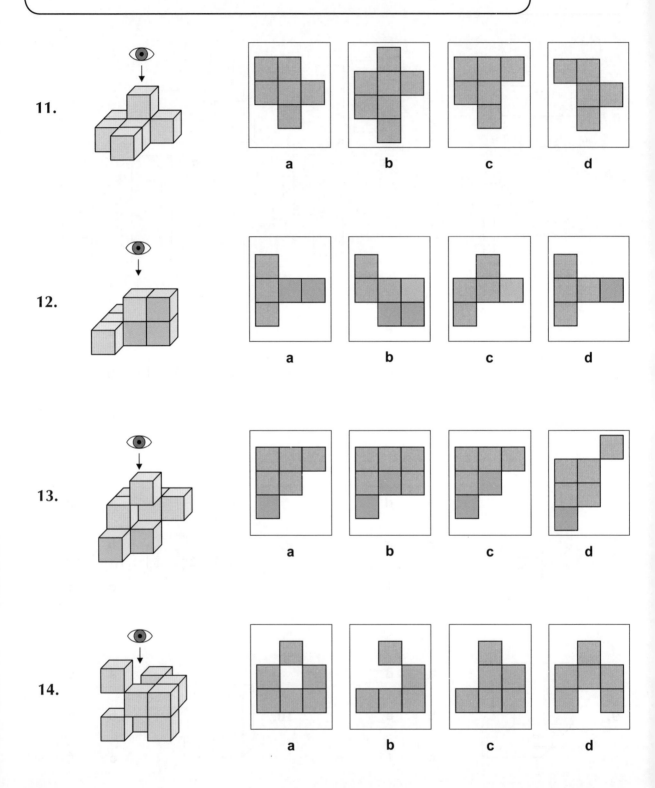

11.

a   b   c   d

12.

a   b   c   d

13.

a   b   c   d

14.

a   b   c   d

Work out which of the 3D shapes can be made from the net.

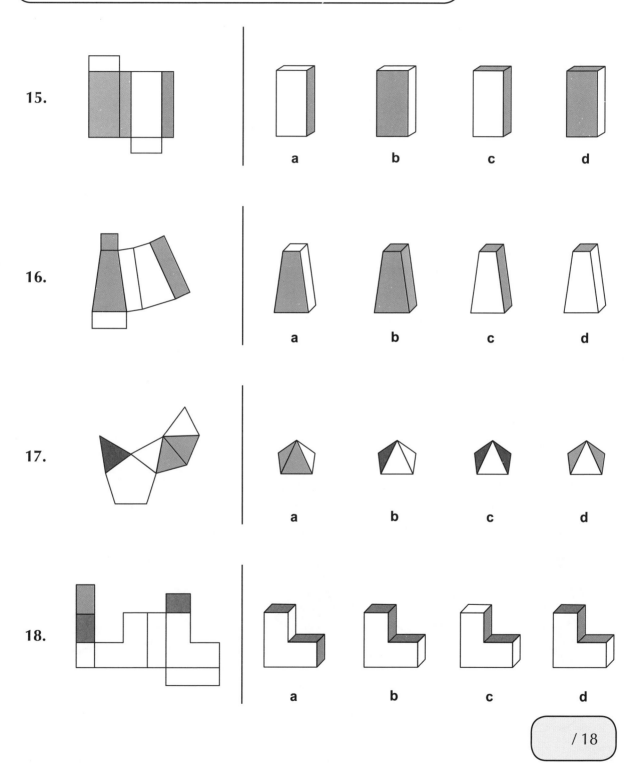

15.

a   b   c   d

16.

a   b   c   d

17.

a   b   c   d

18.

a   b   c   d

/ 18

19   Test 3

Puzzles 1

These puzzles are a brilliant way of practising your **3D views** and **net** skills.

Lost in Rotation

Sally is lost in a strange city.
She uses the two buildings to her left and right to get her bearings.
Circle the letter nearest to her location.

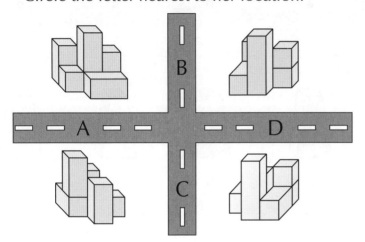

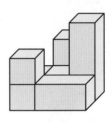

This is the view to Sally's left.

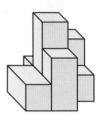

This is the view to Sally's right.

Pyramid Panic

Pharaoh is building a new six-sided pyramid.
Below are three views of the same pyramid.
Each shading appears twice. Complete its net.

You have **10 minutes** to do this test. Circle the letter for each correct answer.

> A square is folded and then a hole is punched, as shown on the left. Work out which option shows the square when unfolded.

1.
a   b   c   d

2. 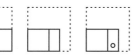
a   b   c   d

3. 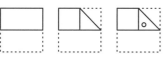
a   b   c   d

4.
a   b   c   d

5.
a   b   c   d

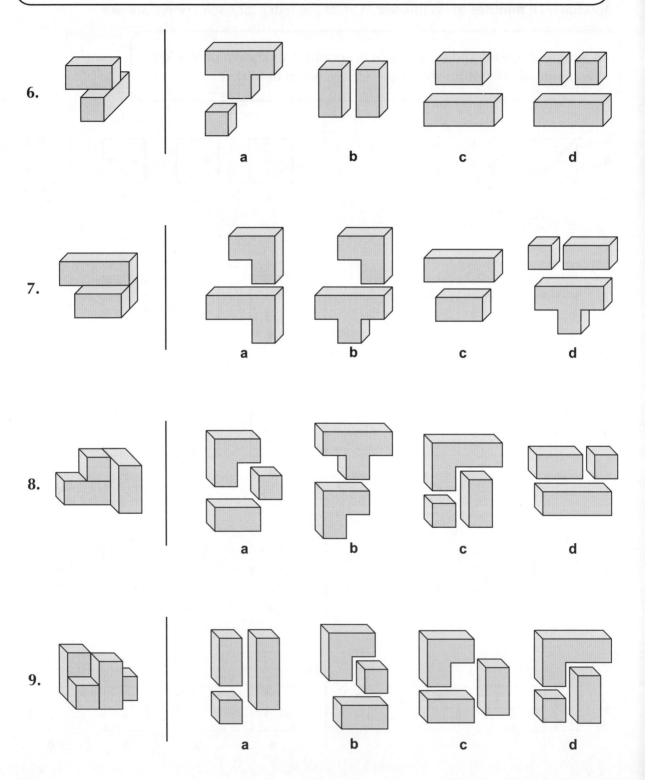

6.

    a   b   c   d

7.

    a   b   c   d

8.

    a   b   c   d

9.

    a   b   c   d

Work out which option is the 3D figure viewed from the **left**.

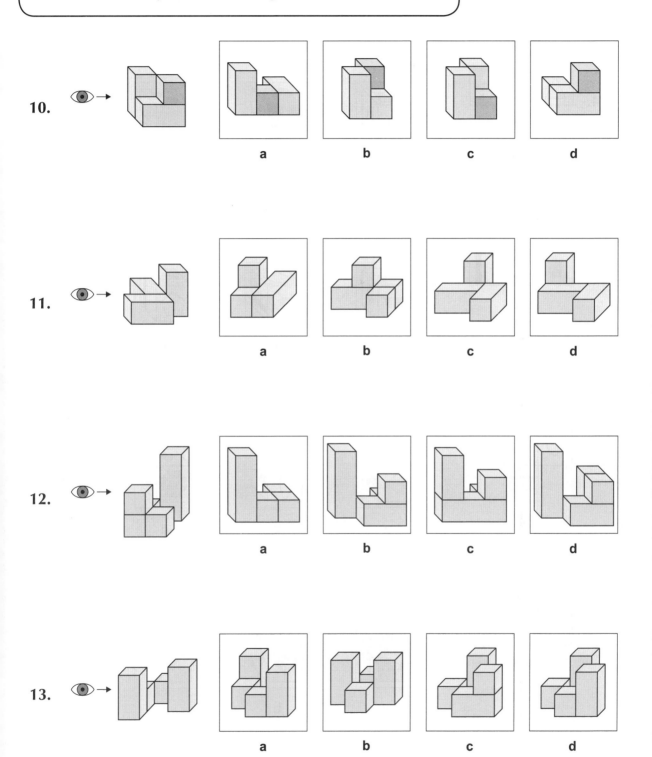

10.

a   b   c   d

11.

a   b   c   d

12.

a   b   c   d

13.

a   b   c   d

Test 4

Work out which of the four cubes can be made from the net.

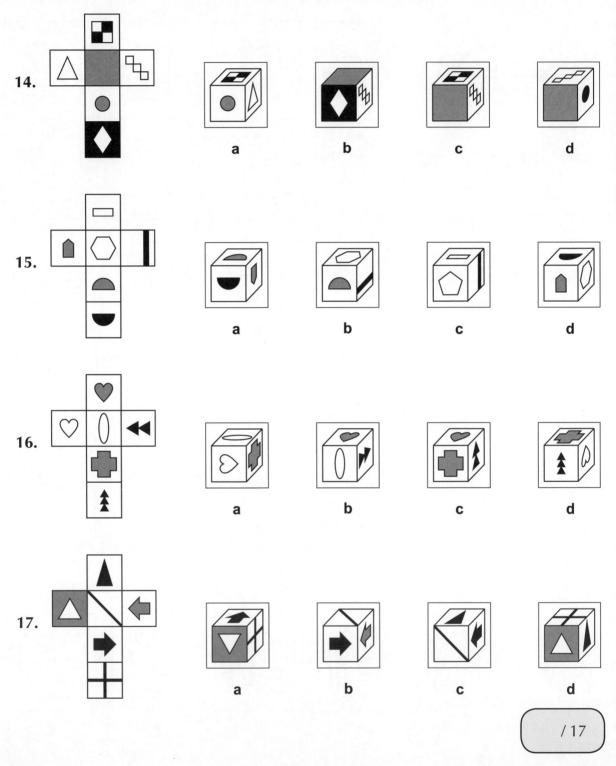

14.

a b c d

15.

a b c d

16.

a b c d

17.

a b c d

/ 17

Test 5

You have **10 minutes** to do this test. Circle the letter for each correct answer.

> A square is folded and then a hole is punched, as shown on the left.
> Work out which option shows the square when unfolded.

1.

a   b   c   d

2.

a   b   c   d

3.

a   b   c   d

4.

a   b   c   d

25

The figures on the left show different views of the same cube. All the cube faces are different. Work out which of the options should replace the blue cube face.

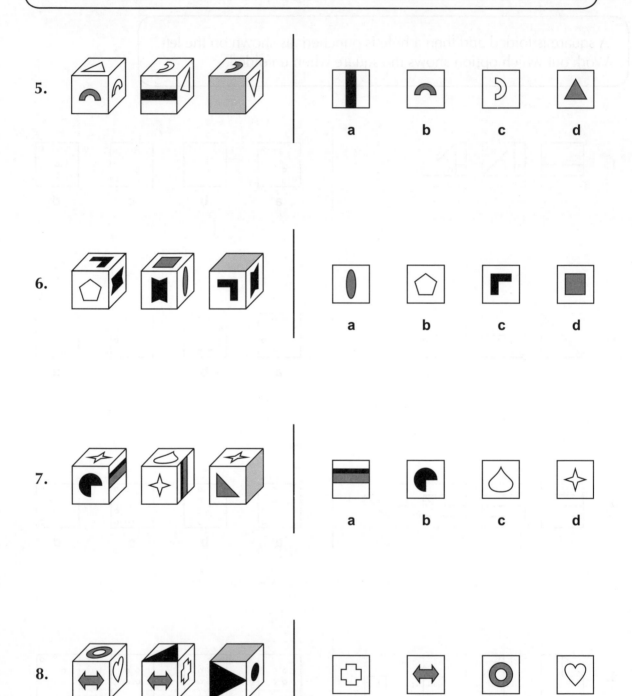

5.

a   b   c   d

6.

a   b   c   d

7.

a   b   c   d

8.

a   b   c   d

Work out which 3D figure in the grey box has been rotated to make the new 3D figure.

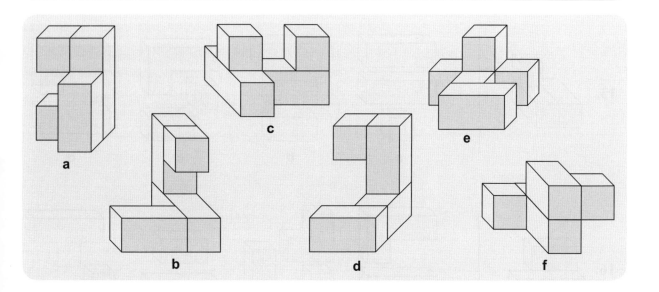

a

c

e

b

d

f

9.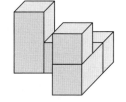

a   d

b   e

c   f

10.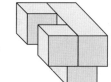

a   d

b   e

c   f

11.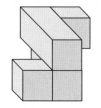

a   d

b   e

c   f

12.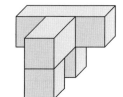

a   d

b   e

c   f

13.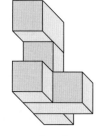

a   d

b   e

c   f

14.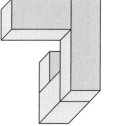

a   d

b   e

c   f

Test 5

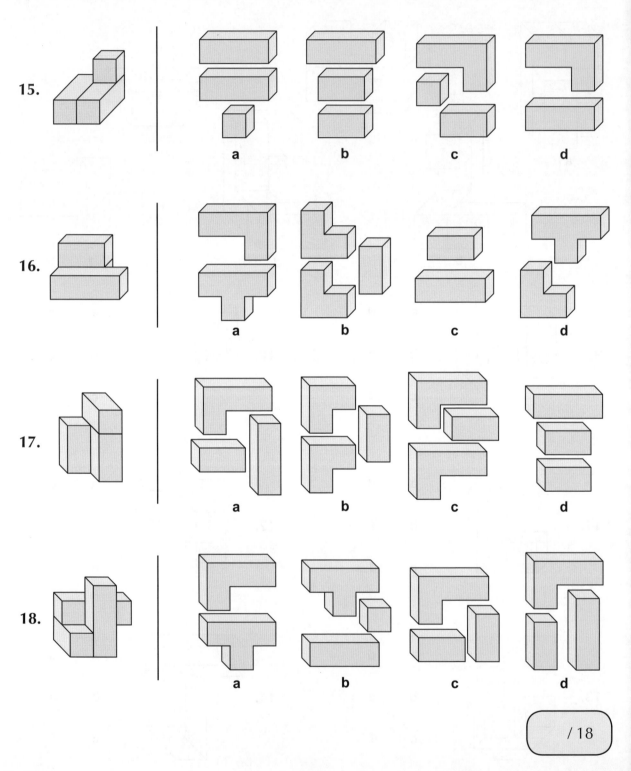

15.

a   b   c   d

16.

a   b   c   d

17.

a   b   c   d

18.

a   b   c   d

/ 18

28

Test 6

You have **10 minutes** to do this test. Circle the letter for each correct answer.

Work out which option is a 2D view from **above** the 3D figure shown.

1.

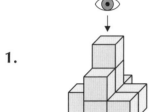

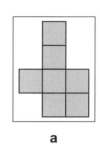 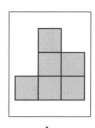 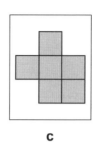 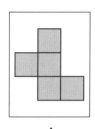

a   b   c   d

2.

 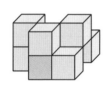

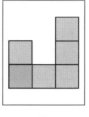 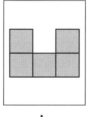 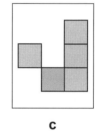 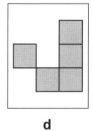

a   b   c   d

3.

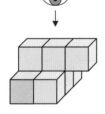

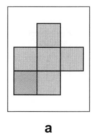 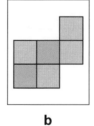 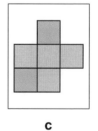 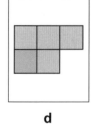

a   b   c   d

4.

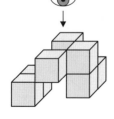

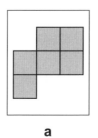 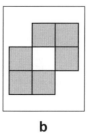 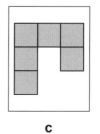 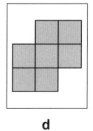

a   b   c   d

29

Work out which option can be put together with the
figure on the left to make the 3D shape in the grey box.

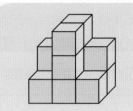

5.

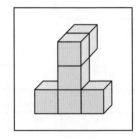

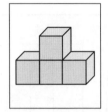
a

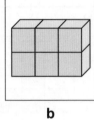
b

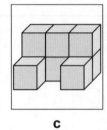
c

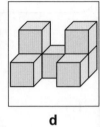
d

6.

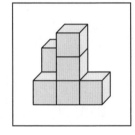

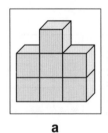
a

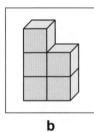
b

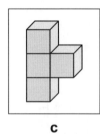
c

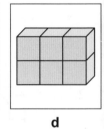
d

7.

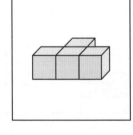

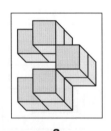
a

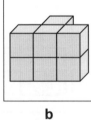
b

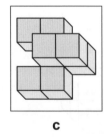
c

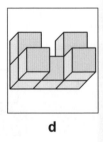
d

8.

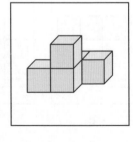

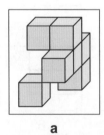
a

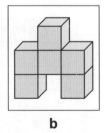
b

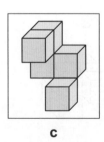
c

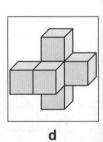
d

Work out which of the four cubes can be made from the net.

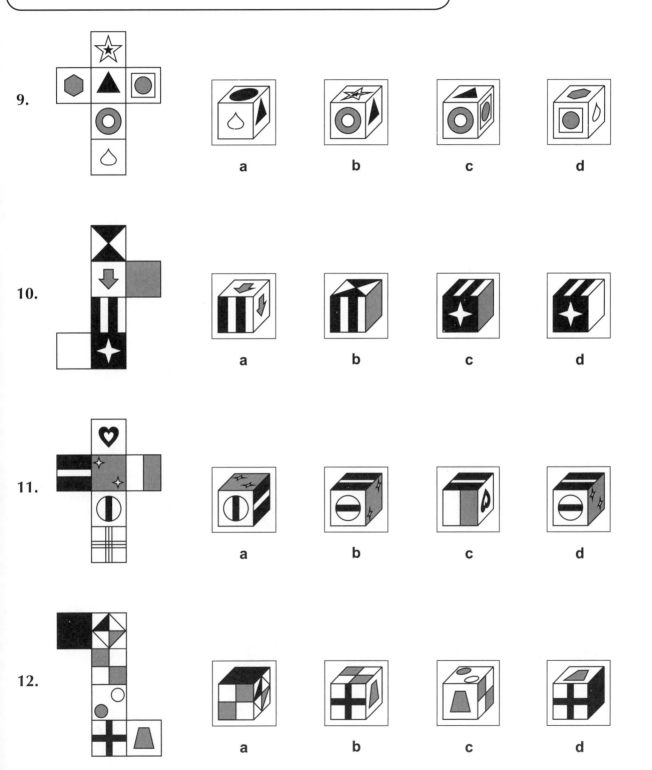

9.

a   b   c   d

10.

a   b   c   d

11.

a   b   c   d

12.

a   b   c   d

Work out which option shows the figure on the left when folded along the dotted line.

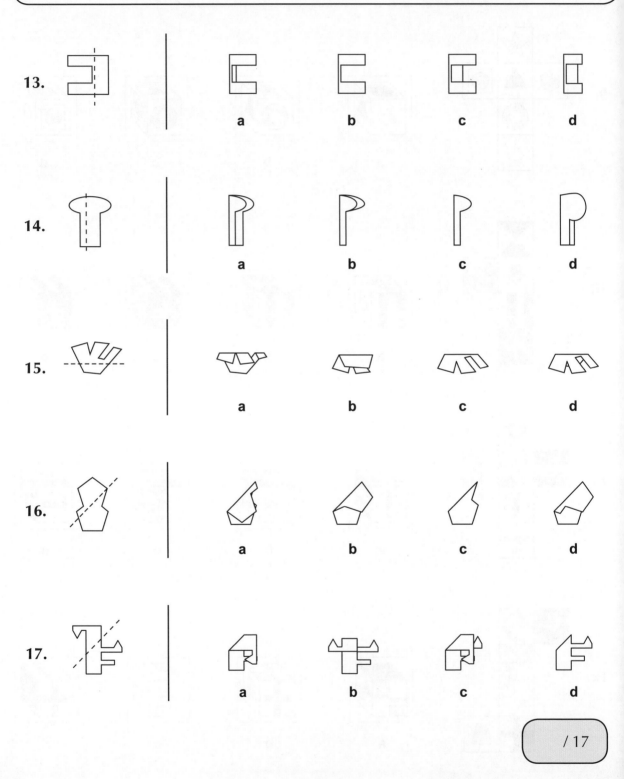

13.
    a   b   c   d

14.
    a   b   c   d

15.
    a   b   c   d

16.
    a   b   c   d

17.
    a   b   c   d

/ 17

Puzzles 2

That's the second block of tests done. Now for something a bit different.

Cube Conundrum

Robin is making two identical children's puzzles. In each puzzle, eight cubes fit together to make a larger cube with a picture on each face.

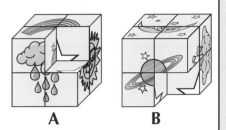

A   B

Which of the nets below will form the final cubes in puzzles A and B?

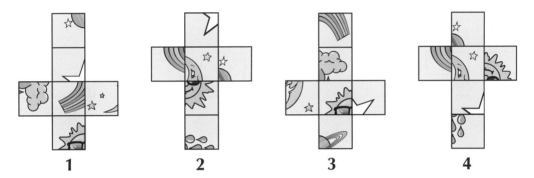

1   2   3   4

Folded Fox

Molly is folding a square piece of paper to form a fox's head. Here are the instructions she is following:

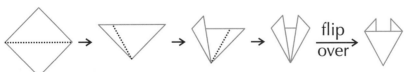

Molly wants to draw the fox's eyes and nose on the paper before she folds it. Which of the following shows the correct positions?

A

B

C

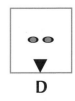

D

You have **10 minutes** to do this test. Circle the letter for each correct answer.

> A square is folded and then a hole is punched, as shown on the left.
> Work out which option shows the square when unfolded.

1.

   a   **b**   **c**   **d**

2.

   a   **b**   **c**   **d**

3.

   a   **b**   **c**   **d**

4.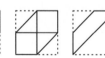

   a   **b**   **c**   **d**

5.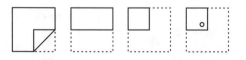

   a   **b**   **c**   **d**

Work out which of the 3D shapes can be made from the net.

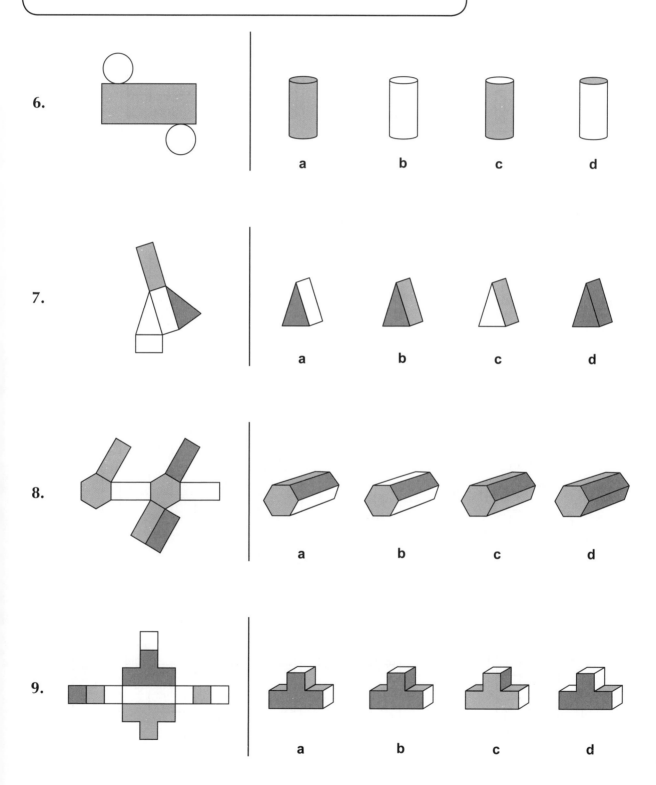

6.

a   b   c   d

7.

a   b   c   d

8.

a   b   c   d

9.

a   b   c   d

Work out which option is a 2D view from the **right** of the 3D figure shown.

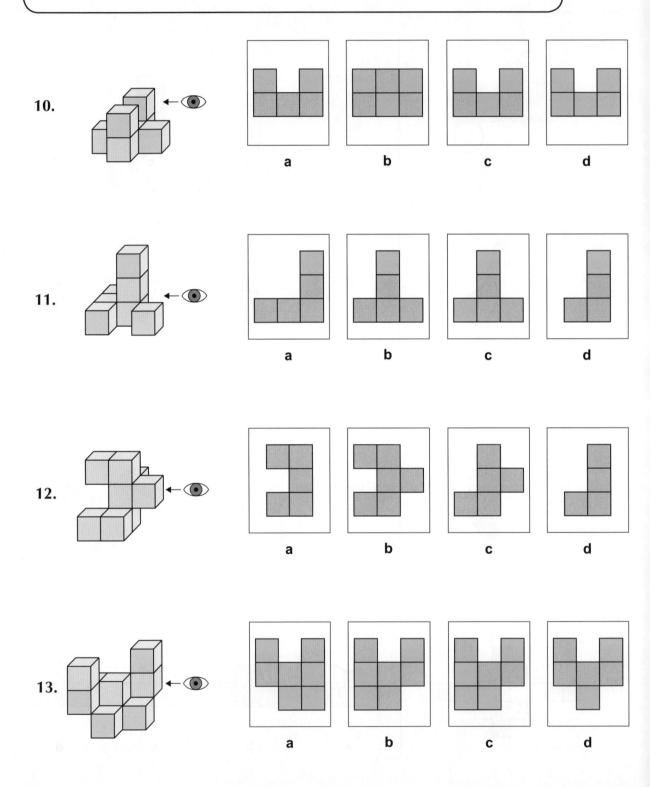

10.

a b c d

11.

a b c d

12.

a b c d

13.

a b c d

36

Work out which 3D figure in the grey box has been rotated to make the new 3D figure.

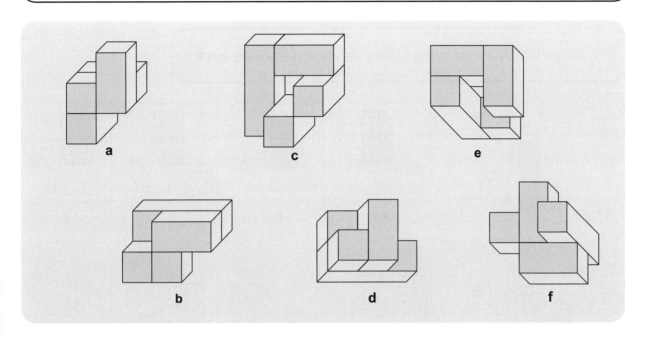

a

c

e

b

d

f

14.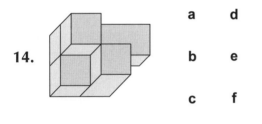

a	d
b	e
c	f

15.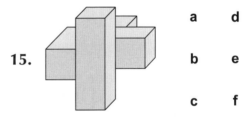

a	d
b	e
c	f

16.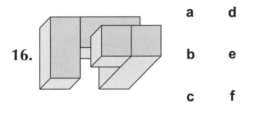

a	d
b	e
c	f

17.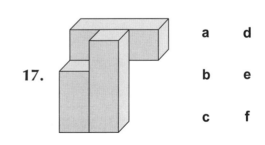

a	d
b	e
c	f

/ 17

Test 7

You have **10 minutes** to do this test. Circle the letter for each correct answer.

Work out which option is the 3D figure viewed from the **back**.

1.

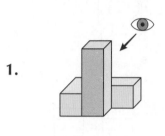

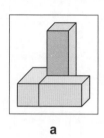

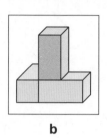

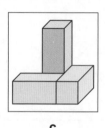

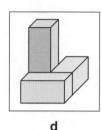

a   b   c   d

2.

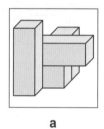

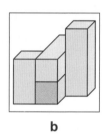

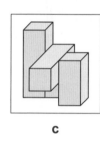

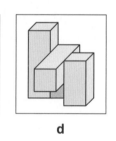

a   b   c   d

3.

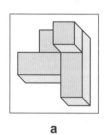

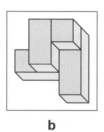

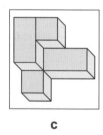

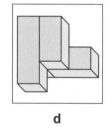

a   b   c   d

4.

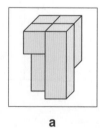

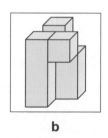

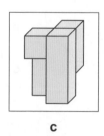

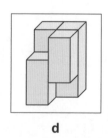

a   b   c   d

Work out which option shows the figure on the left when folded along the dotted line.

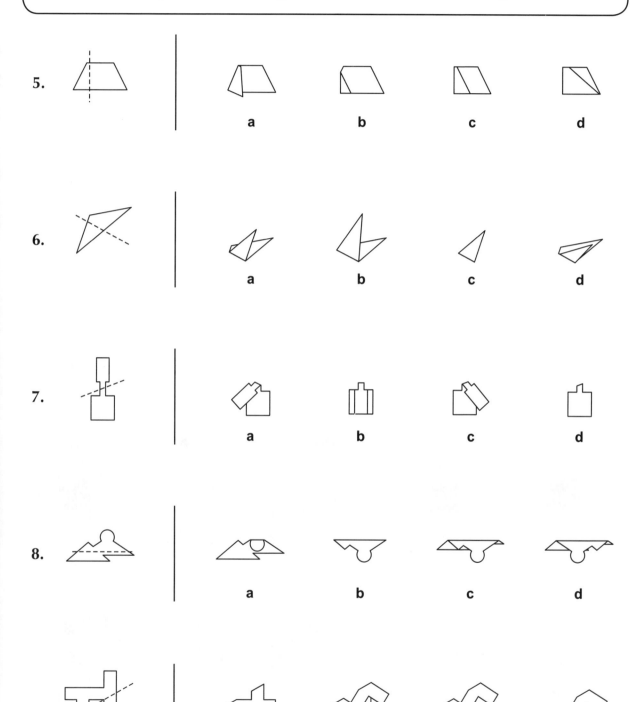

5.

a   b   c   d

6.

a   b   c   d

7.

a   b   c   d

8.

a   b   c   d

9.

a   b   c   d

39

Work out which of the four partial nets can be folded to make the cube on the left.

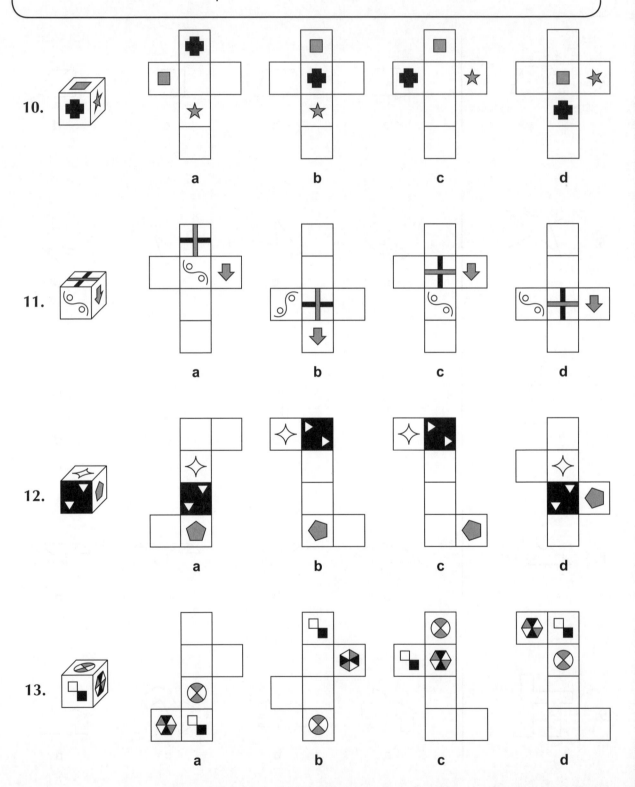

10.

a   b   c   d

11.

a   b   c   d

12.

a   b   c   d

13.

a   b   c   d

Work out which option can be put together with the figure on the left to make the 3D shape in the grey box.

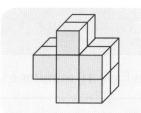

14. 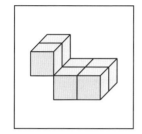   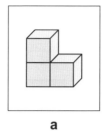      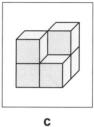   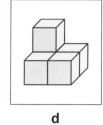

                    a   **b**   **c**   **d**

15. 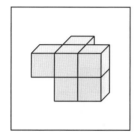   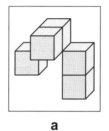   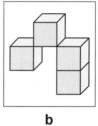   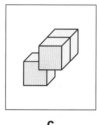   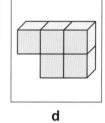

                    a   **b**   **c**   **d**

16. 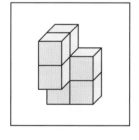   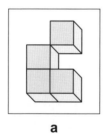   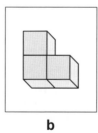   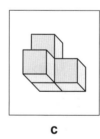   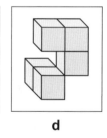

                    a   **b**   **c**   **d**

17. 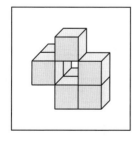   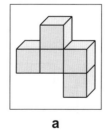   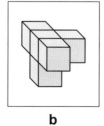   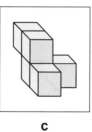   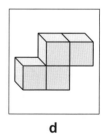

                    a   **b**   **c**   **d**

/ 17

Test 8

⏱ 10

You have **10 minutes** to do this test. Circle the letter for each correct answer.

Work out which option is a 2D view from the **back** of the 3D figure shown.

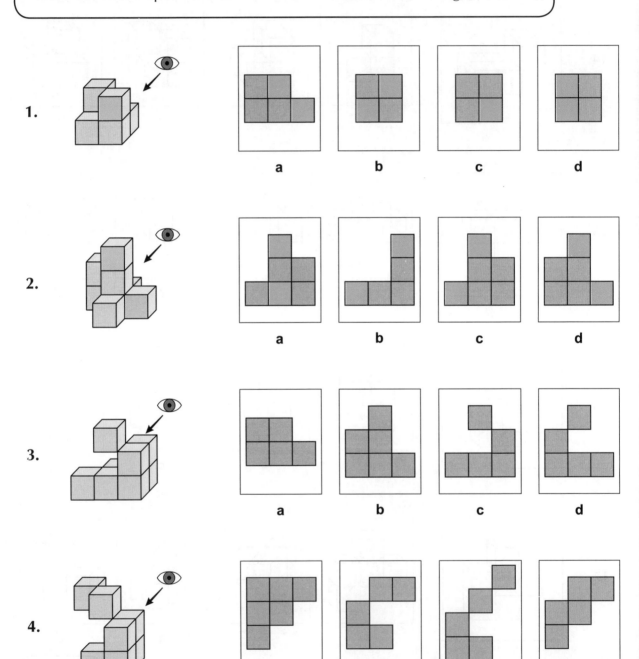

1.

a   b   c   d

2.

a   b   c   d

3.

a   b   c   d

4.

a   b   c   d

Work out which of the four cubes can be made from the net.

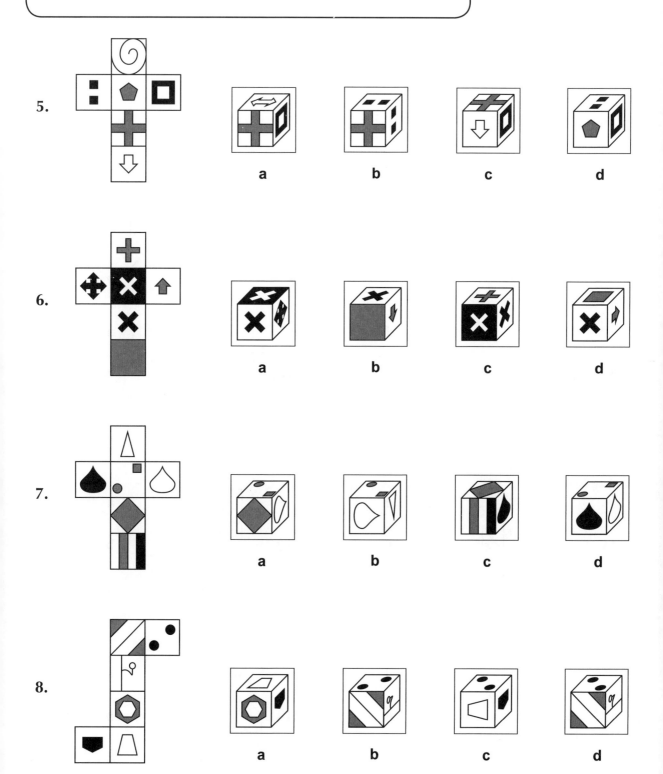

5.   a   b   c   d

6.   a   b   c   d

7.   a   b   c   d

8.   a   b   c   d

43

Work out which 3D figure in the grey box has been rotated to make the new 3D figure.

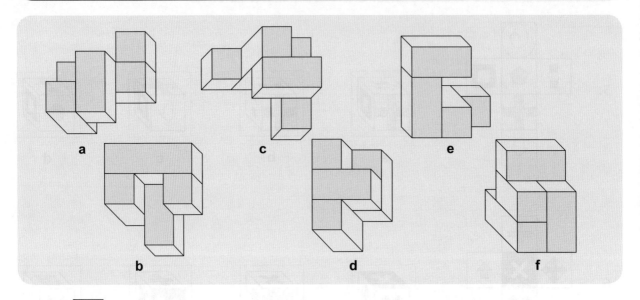

a

c

e

b

d

f

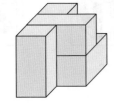

9.

a	d
b	e
c	f

10.

a	d
b	e
c	f

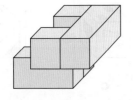

11.

a	d
b	e
c	f

12.

a	d
b	e
c	f

13.

a	d
b	e
c	f

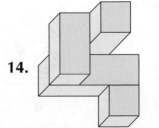

14.

a	d
b	e
c	f

Work out which set of blocks can be put together to make the 3D figure on the left.

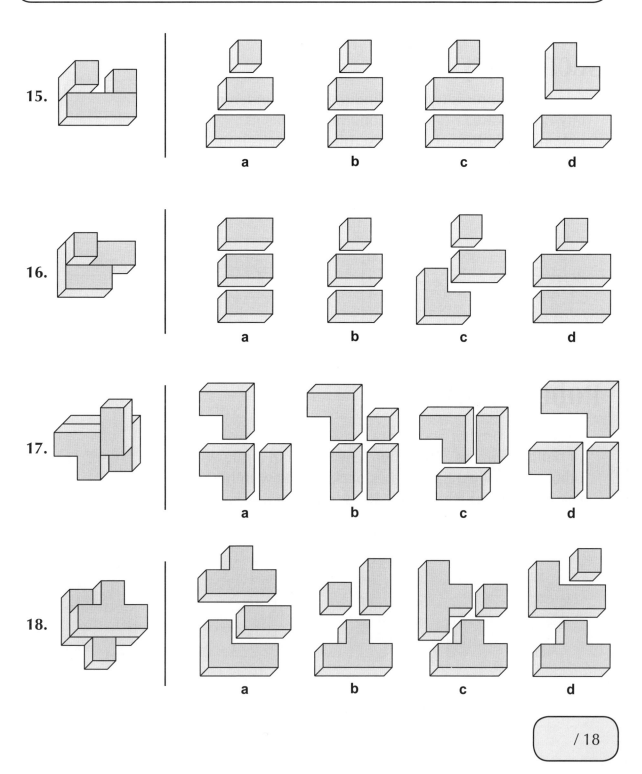

15.

a   b   c   d

16.

a   b   c   d

17.

a   b   c   d

18.

a   b   c   d

/ 18

This feels like a good time to practise your **2D views** and **rotating 3D shapes** skills.

Secret City

Eric the Explorer is trying to find the secret underground city of Blockadia. A stone monument marks its entrance. He has an ancient scroll which tells him what this monument looks like from above. Eric has found four monuments. Which is the right one?

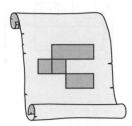

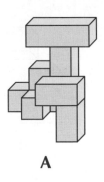

A

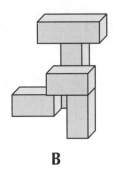

B

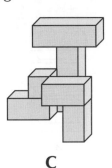

C

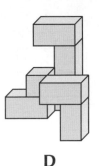

D

Robot Riddle

Saskia, her brother and her two sisters each make a robot out of building blocks. They then leave them in a pile with their other toys. When Saskia goes back to play with her robot, she isn't sure which is hers. Work out which is Saskia's robot.

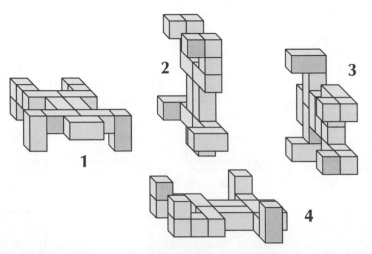

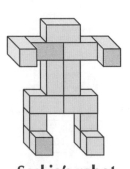

Saskia's robot

Test 10

You have **10 minutes** to do this test. Circle the letter for each correct answer.

> The figures on the left show different views of the same cube. All the cube faces are different. Work out which of the options should replace the blue cube face.

1. |

                                                  a   b   c   d

2. |

                                                  a   b   c   d

3. |

                                                  a   b   c   d

4. |

                                                  a   b   c   d

Work out which 3D figure in the grey box has been rotated to make the new 3D figure.

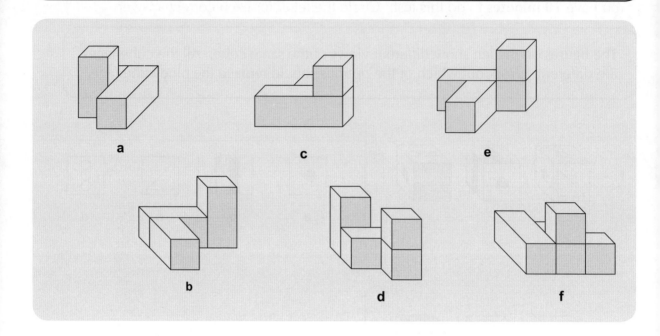

a

c

e

b

d

f

5.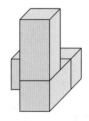

a   d

b   e

c   f

6.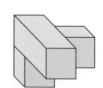

a   d

b   e

c   f

7.

a   d

b   e

c   f

8.

a   d

b   e

c   f

A square is folded and then a hole is punched, as shown on the left.
Work out which option shows the square when unfolded.

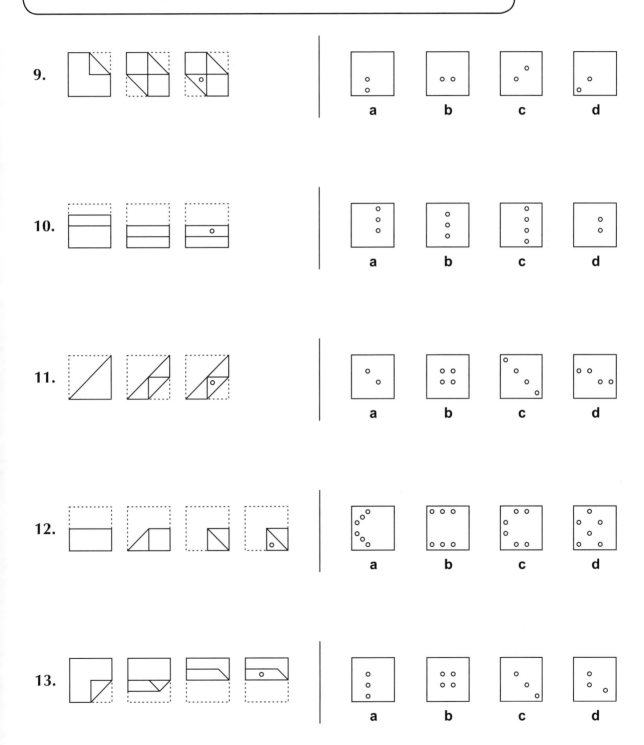

9.

          a   b   c   d

10.

          a   b   c   d

11.

          a   b   c   d

12.

          a   b   c   d

13.

          a   b   c   d

Work out which option is a 2D view from the **right** of the 3D figure shown.

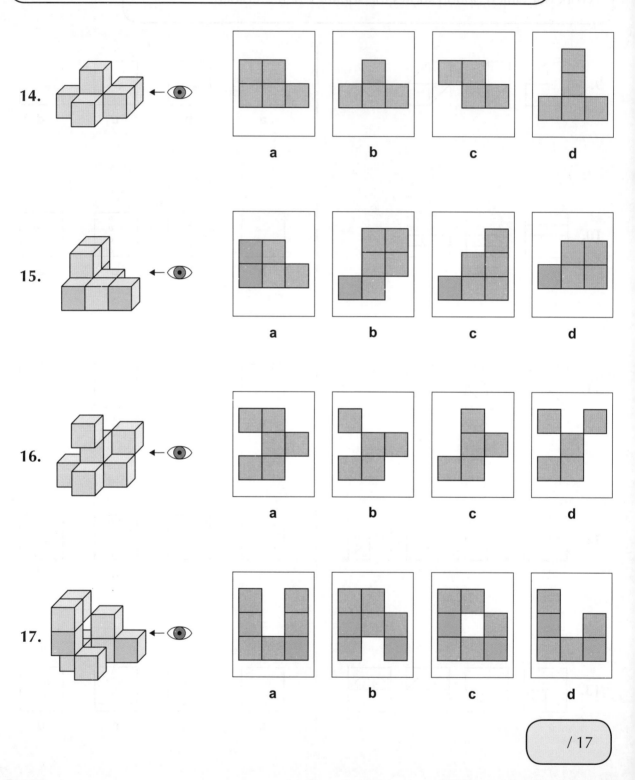

14.

a   b   c   d

15.

a   b   c   d

16.

a   b   c   d

17.

a   b   c   d

/ 17

You have **10 minutes** to do this test. Circle the letter for each correct answer.

Work out which option shows the figure on the left when folded along the dotted line.

1. 　　　　　　

　　　　a　　　　　b　　　　　c　　　　　d

2. 　　　　　　

　　　　a　　　　　b　　　　　c　　　　　d

3. 　　　　　　

　　　　a　　　　　b　　　　　c　　　　　d

4. 　　　　　　

　　　　a　　　　　b　　　　　c　　　　　d

5.

　　　　a　　　　　b　　　　　c　　　　　d

Work out which option is the 3D figure viewed from the **left**.

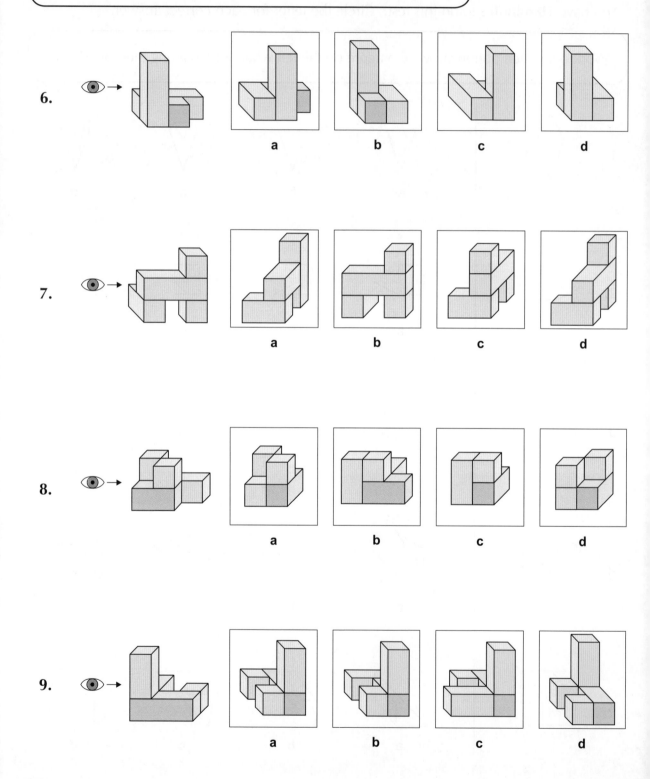

6.

a b c d

7.

a b c d

8.

a b c d

9.

a b c d

52

Work out which of the 3D shapes can be made from the net.

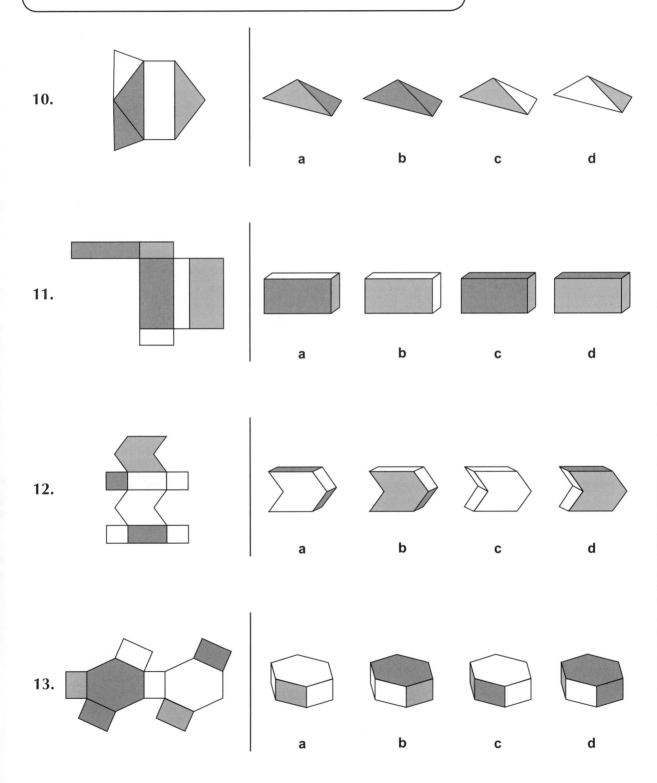

10.   a   b   c   d

11.   a   b   c   d

12.   a   b   c   d

13.   a   b   c   d

53

Work out which option can be put together with the figure on the left to make the 3D shape in the grey box.

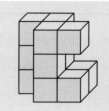

14.
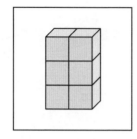
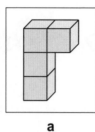
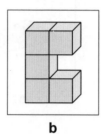
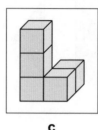
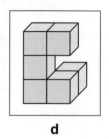

a b c d

15.
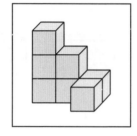
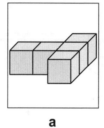
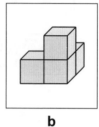
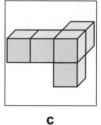
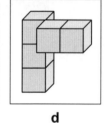

a b c d

16.
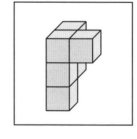
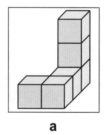
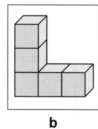
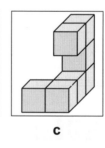
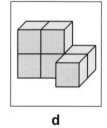

a b c d

17.
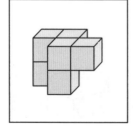
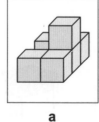
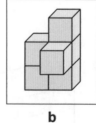
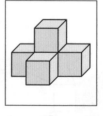
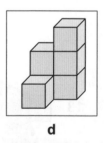

a b c d

/ 17

54

Test 12

You have **10 minutes** to do this test. Circle the letter for each correct answer.

Work out which 3D figure in the grey box has been rotated to make the new 3D figure.

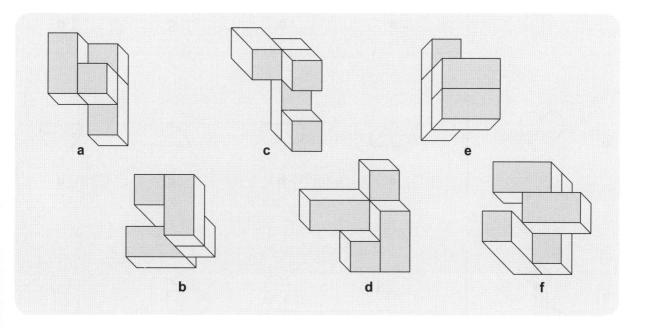

a

c

e

b

d

f

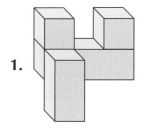

1.

a	d
b	e
c	f

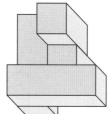

2.

a	d
b	e
c	f

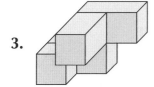

3.

a	d
b	e
c	f

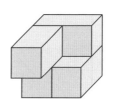

4.

a	d
b	e
c	f

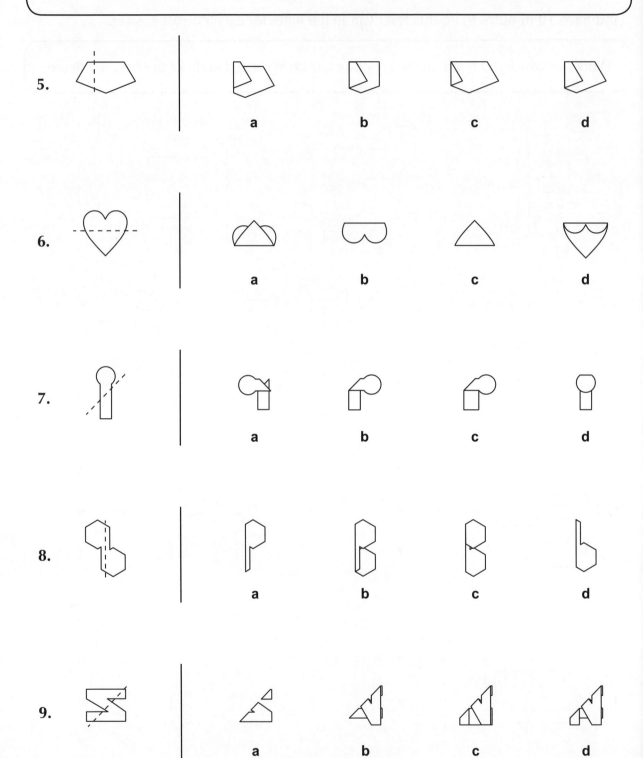

5.   a   b   c   d

6.   a   b   c   d

7.   a   b   c   d

8.   a   b   c   d

9.   a   b   c   d

56

Work out which option can be put together with the figure on the left to make the 3D shape in the grey box.

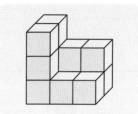

10.

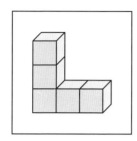

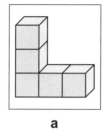
a

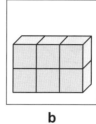
b

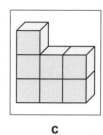
c

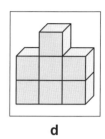
d

11.

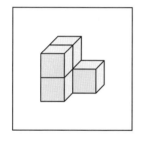

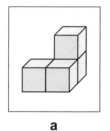
a

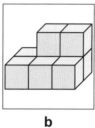
b

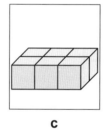
c

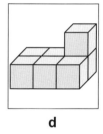
d

12.

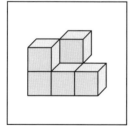

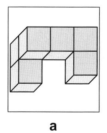
a

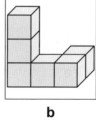
b

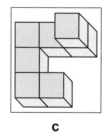
c

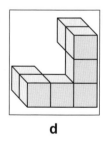
d

13.

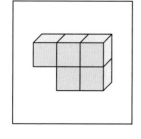

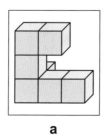
a

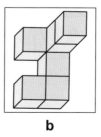
b

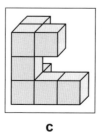
c

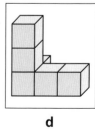
d

Test 12

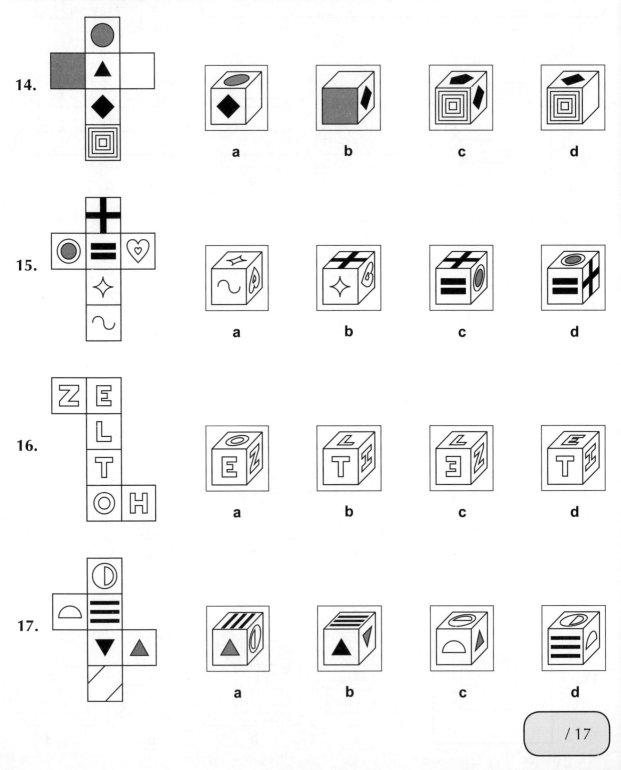

Work out which of the four cubes can be made from the net.

14.

a b c d

15.

a b c d

16.

a b c d

17.

a b c d

/ 17

Puzzles 4

Time for fun with some more puzzles — these ones will help your **fold and punch** skills.

Folding and Holding (Hands)

Tobias is making paper dolls. He folds each rectangular piece of paper three times and then cuts out a shape. Circle the paper dolls Tobias makes.

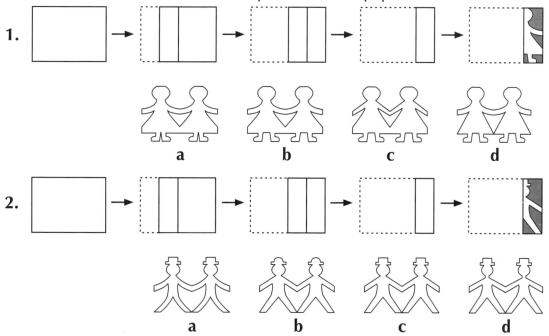

Tobias tries folding a circular piece of paper three times instead and then cuts out a shape. Circle the paper dolls Tobias makes.

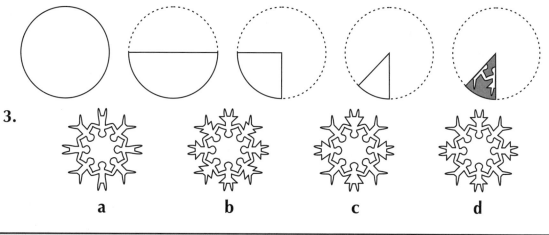

You have **10 minutes** to do this test. Circle the letter for each correct answer.

Work out which option shows the figure on the left when folded along the dotted line.

1.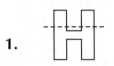

      a   b   c   d

2.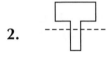

      a   b   c   d

3.

      a   b   c   d

4.

      a   b   c   d

5.

      a   b   c   d

60

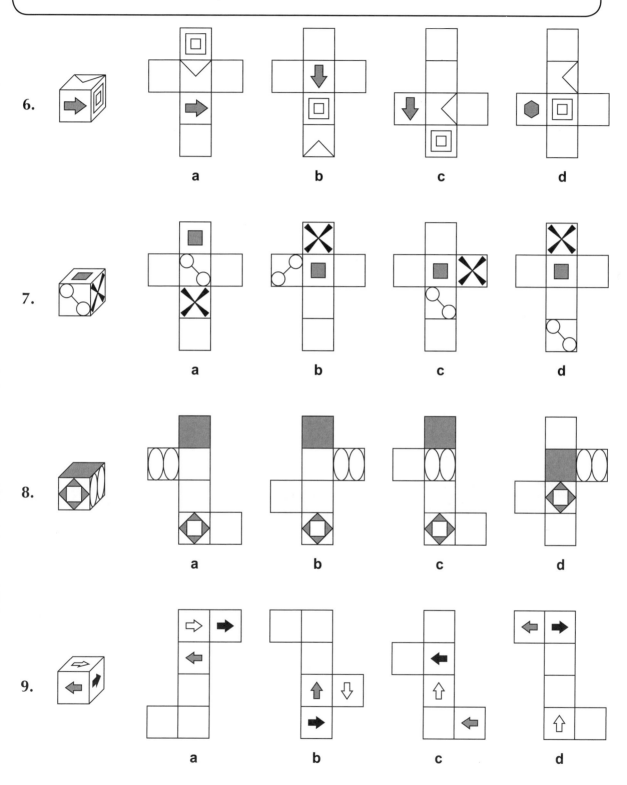

6. a b c d

7. a b c d

8. a b c d

9. a b c d

The figures on the left show different views of the same cube. All the cube faces are different. Work out which of the options should replace the blue cube face.

10.

a	b	c	d

11.

a	b	c	d

12.

a	b	c	d

13.

a	b	c	d

Work out which option is the 3D figure viewed from the **right**.

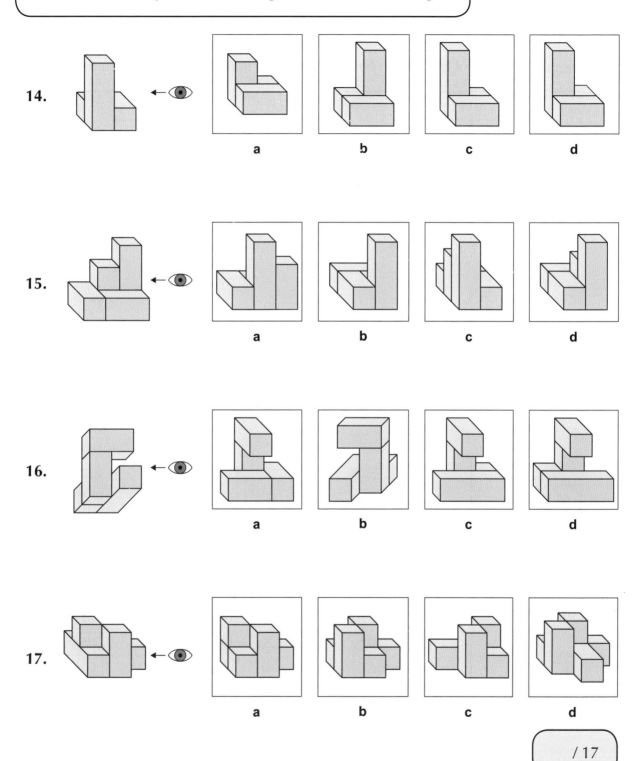

14.

a   b   c   d

15.

a   b   c   d

16.

a   b   c   d

17.

a   b   c   d

/ 17

Test 14

You have **10 minutes** to do this test. Circle the letter for each correct answer.

Work out which set of blocks can be put together to make the 3D figure on the left.

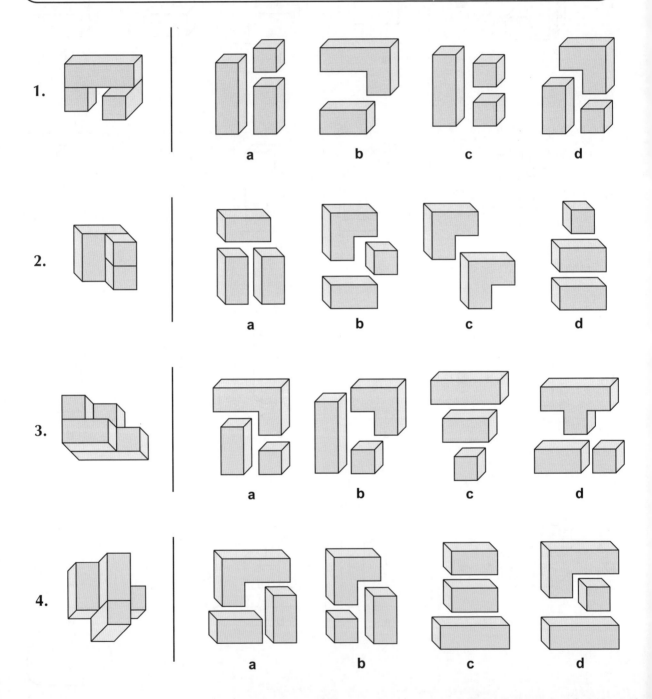

Test 14

64

© CGP — not to be photocopied

Work out which 3D figure in the grey box has been rotated to make the new 3D figure.

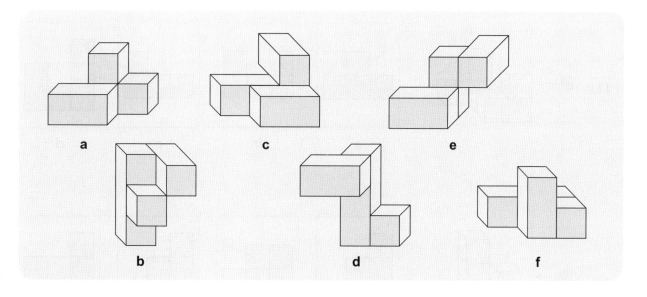

a

c

e

b

d

f

5.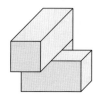

a	d
b	e
c	f

6.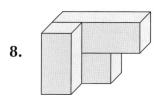

a	d
b	e
c	f

7.

a	d
b	e
c	f

8.

a	d
b	e
c	f

9.

a	d
b	e
c	f

10.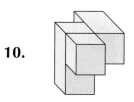

a	d
b	e
c	f

Test 14

Work out which option is a 2D view from the **left** of the 3D figure shown.

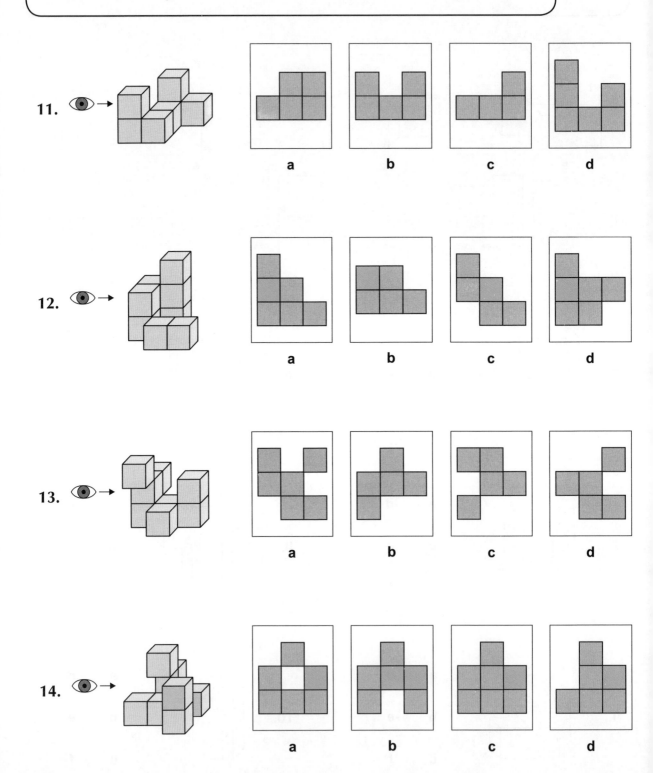

11.

a   b   c   d

12.

a   b   c   d

13.

a   b   c   d

14.

a   b   c   d

Work out which of the four cubes can be made from the net.

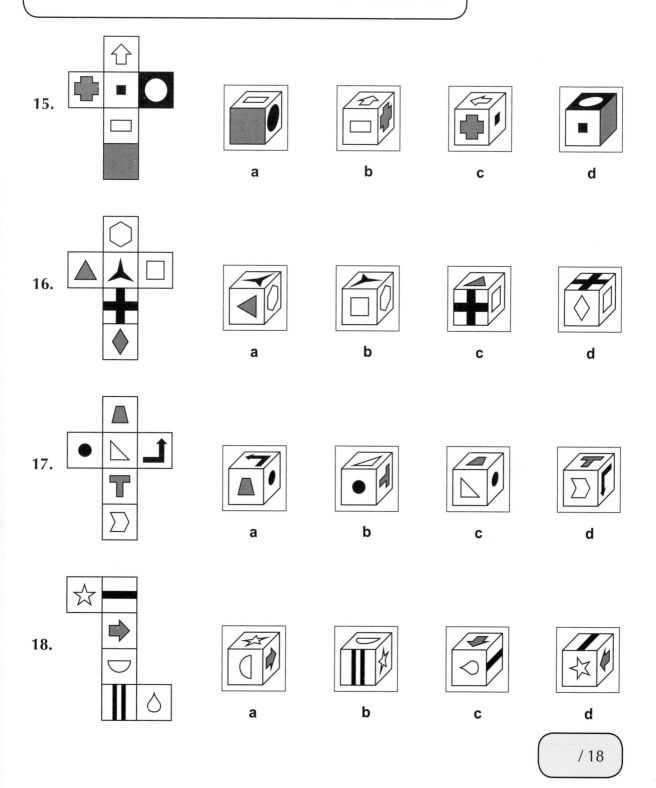

15.   a   b   c   d

16.   a   b   c   d

17.   a   b   c   d

18.   a   b   c   d

/ 18

Test 14

Test 15

You have **10 minutes** to do this test. Circle the letter for each correct answer.

A square is folded and then a hole is punched, as shown on the left.
Work out which option shows the square when unfolded.

1.
 a   b   c   d

2.
 a   b   c   d

3.
 a   b   c   d

4.
 a   b   c   d

5.
 a   b   c   d

68 © CGP — not to be photocopied

Work out which option is the 3D figure viewed from the **back**.

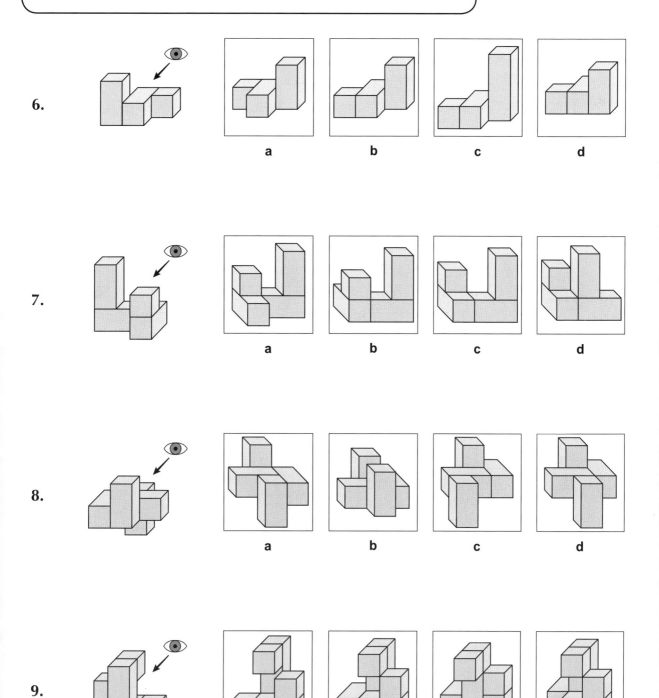

6.

a

b

c

d

7.

a

b

c

d

8.

a

b

c

d

9.

a

b

c

d

Test 15

Work out which set of blocks can be put together to make the 3D figure on the left.

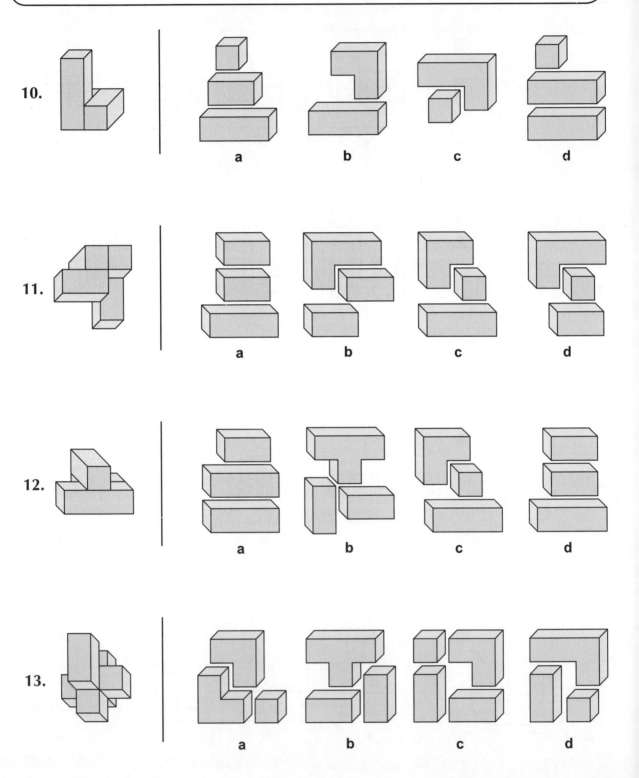

10.

a　　b　　c　　d

11.

a　　b　　c　　d

12.

a　　b　　c　　d

13.

a　　b　　c　　d

Work out which of the 3D shapes can be made from the net.

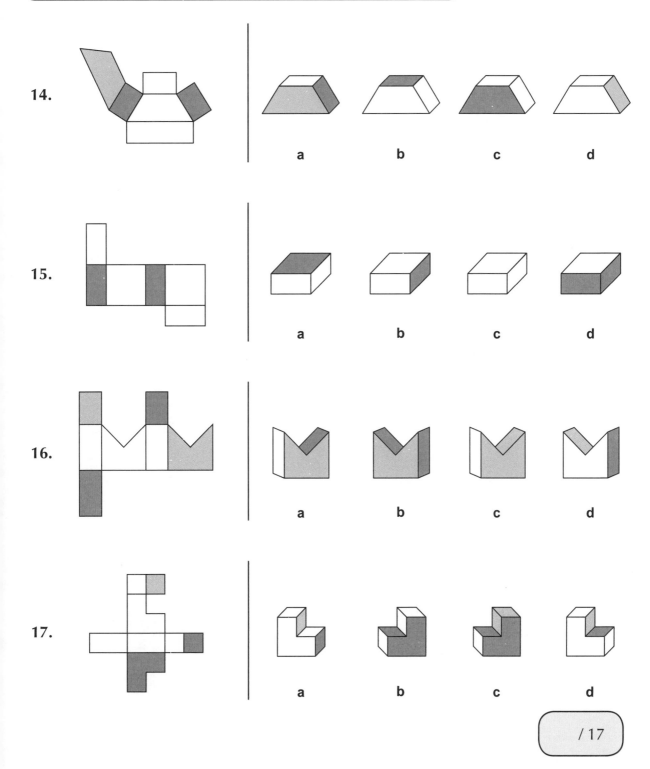

14.

a   b   c   d

15.

a   b   c   d

16.

a   b   c   d

17.

a   b   c   d

/ 17

Test 15

Now it's time for some puzzles. Practise your **complete the shape** and **2D view** skills.

Creepy Crawlies

Rishi is designing a computer game. It features the insect shown below.
The insect can turn left and right in the game.
If the insect is turned 90 degrees from right to left, what will it look like?

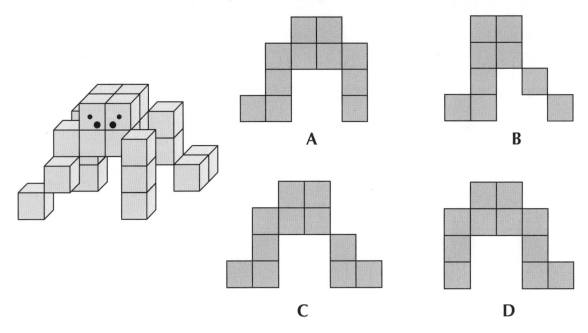

A

B

C

D

Castle Catastrophe

Alice has built the walls of a castle out of
cubes, but her younger brother has broken it.
It had four lines of symmetry.
How many cubes does Alice need to repair it?

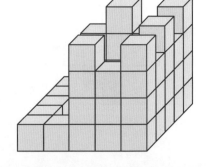

72

10

You have **10 minutes** to do this test. Circle the letter for each correct answer.

Work out which option is a 2D view from the **back** of the 3D figure shown.

1.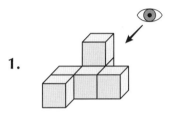

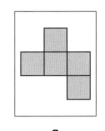 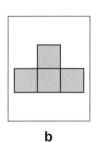 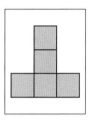 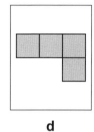

    a   **b**   **c**   **d**

2.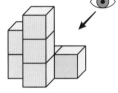

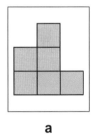 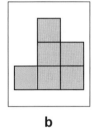 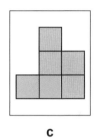 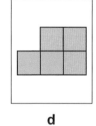

    a   **b**   **c**   **d**

3.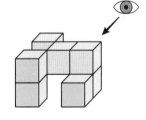

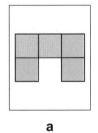 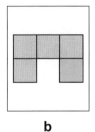 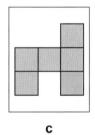 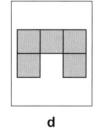

    a   **b**   **c**   **d**

4.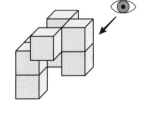

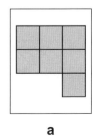 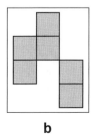 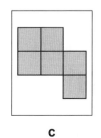 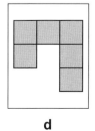

    a   **b**   **c**   **d**

Work out which of the four cubes can be made from the net.

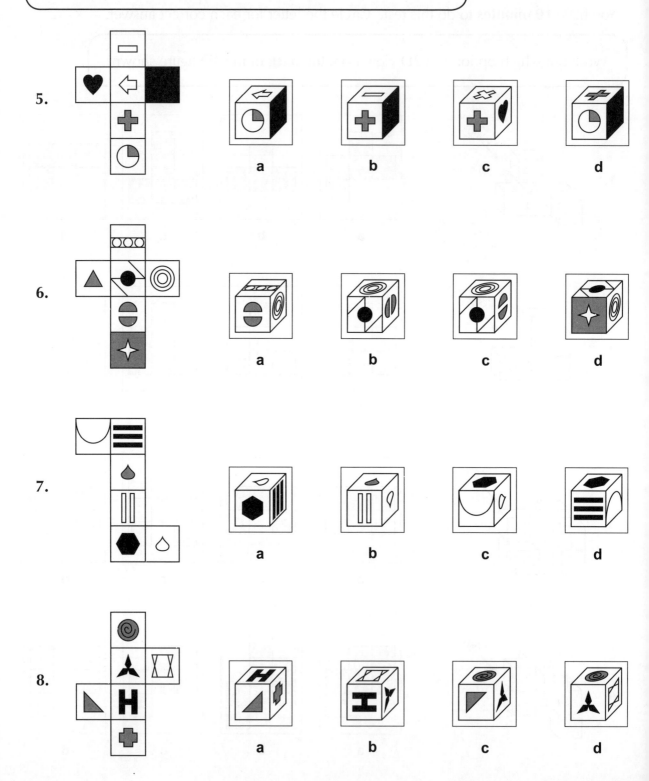

5.   a   b   c   d

6.   a   b   c   d

7.   a   b   c   d

8.   a   b   c   d

Work out which 3D figure in the grey box has been rotated to make the new 3D figure.

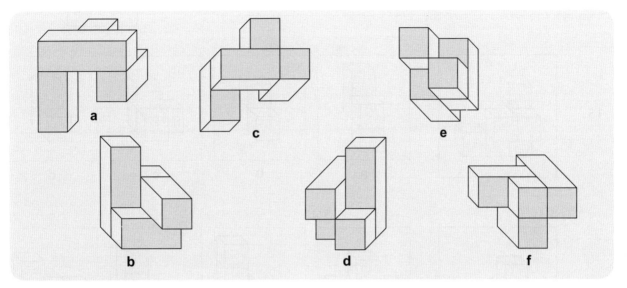

9.
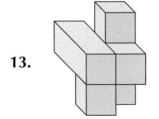

a   d

b   e

c   f

10.

a   d

b   e

c   f

11.
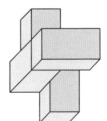

a   d

b   e

c   f

12.

a   d

b   e

c   f

13.
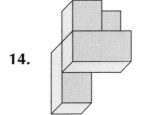

a   d

b   e

c   f

14.

a   d

b   e

c   f

Work out which option can be put together with the figure on the left to make the 3D shape in the grey box.

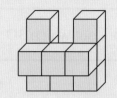

15.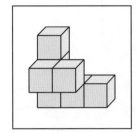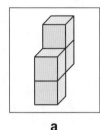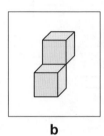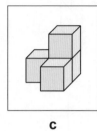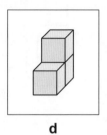

a   b   c   d

16.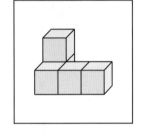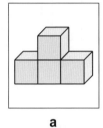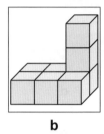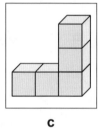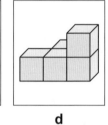

a   b   c   d

17.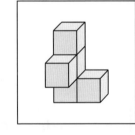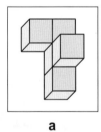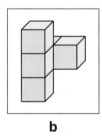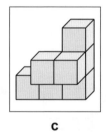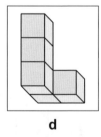

a   b   c   d

18.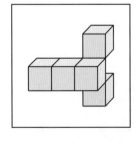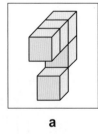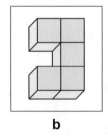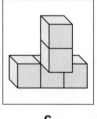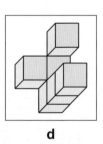

a   b   c   d

/ 18

You have **10 minutes** to do this test. Circle the letter for each correct answer.

Work out which option is the 3D figure viewed from the **right**.

1.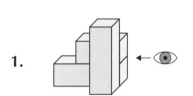

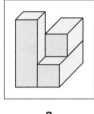 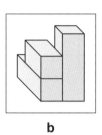 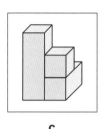 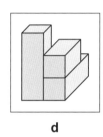

a   b   c   d

2.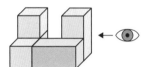

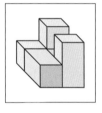 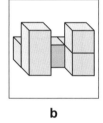 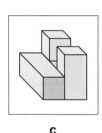 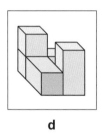

a   b   c   d

3.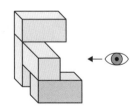

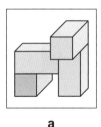 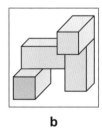 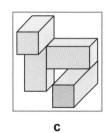 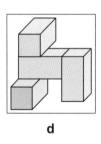

a   b   c   d

4.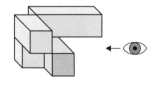

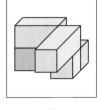 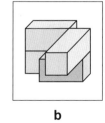 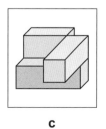 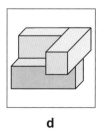

a   b   c   d

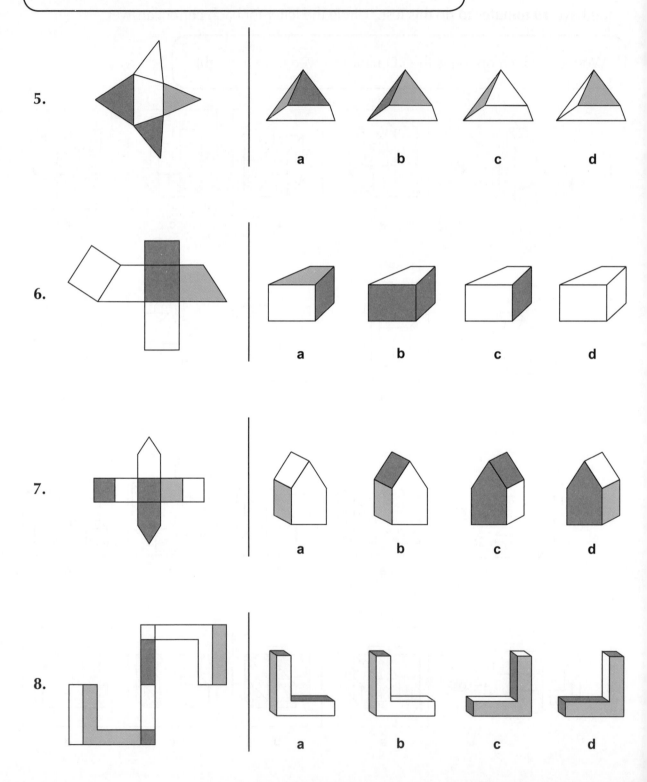

5.

a   b   c   d

6.

a   b   c   d

7.

a   b   c   d

8.

a   b   c   d

The figures on the left show different views of the same cube. All the cube faces are different. Work out which of the options should replace the blue cube face.

9.

      a   b   c   d

10.

      a   b   c   d

11.

      a   b   c   d

12.

      a   b   c   d

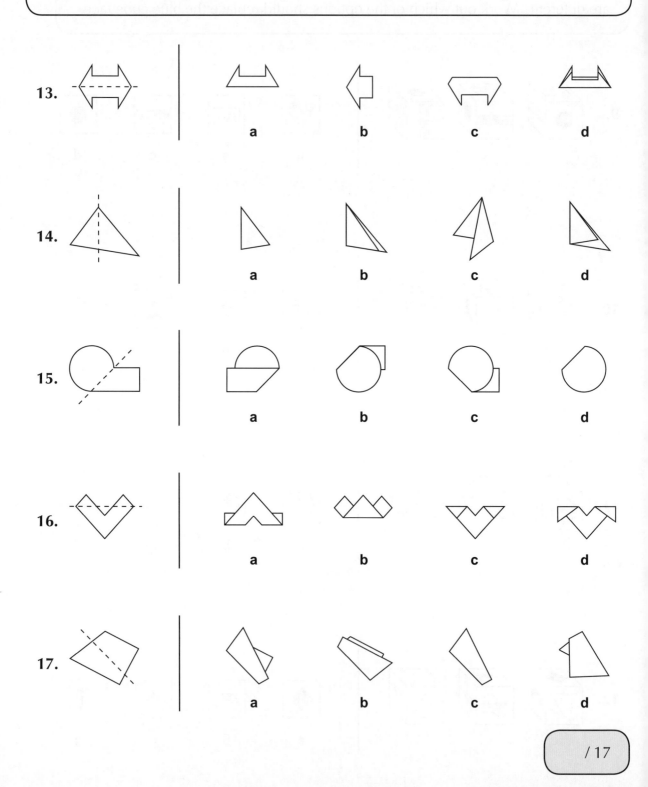

13.   a   b   c   d

14.   a   b   c   d

15.   a   b   c   d

16.   a   b   c   d

17.   a   b   c   d

/ 17

You have **10 minutes** to do this test. Circle the letter for each correct answer.

Work out which 3D figure in the grey box has been rotated to make the new 3D figure.

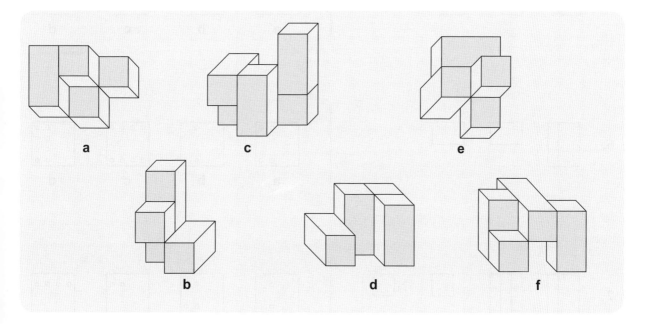

a   c   e

b   d   f

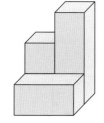

1.

a	d
b	e
c	f

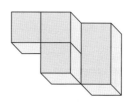

2.

a	d
b	e
c	f

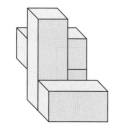

3.

a	d
b	e
c	f

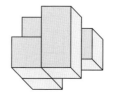

4.

a	d
b	e
c	f

81

A square is folded and then a hole is punched, as shown on the left.
Work out which option shows the square when unfolded.

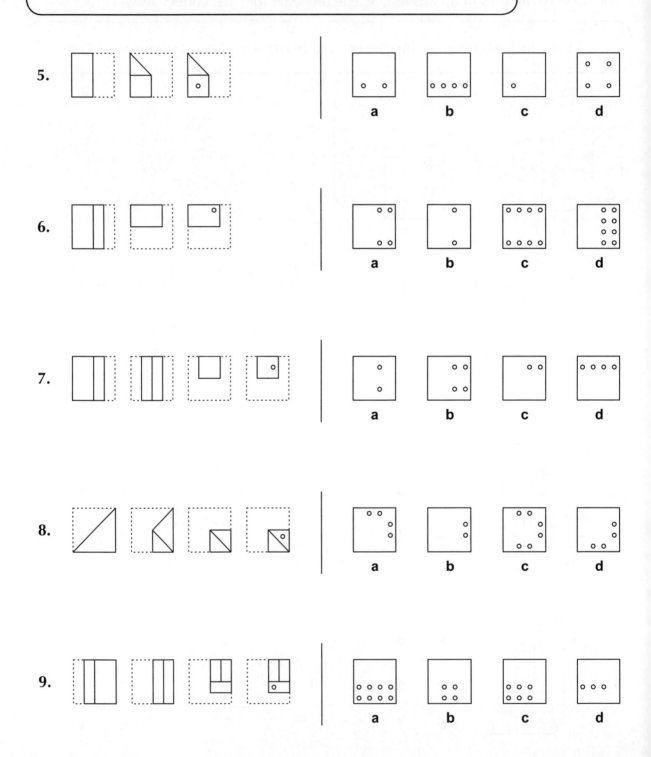

5.

a   b   c   d

6.

a   b   c   d

7.

a   b   c   d

8.

a   b   c   d

9.

a   b   c   d

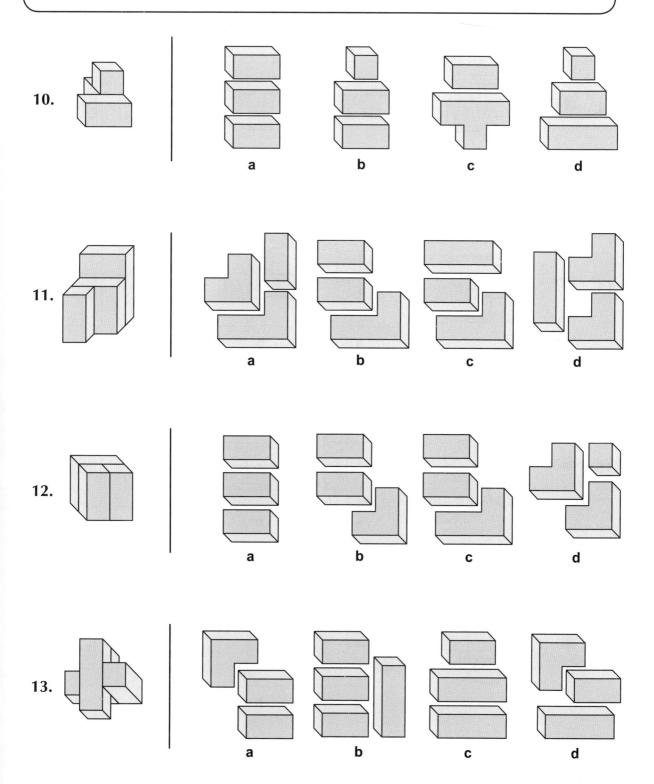

10.

11.

12.

13.

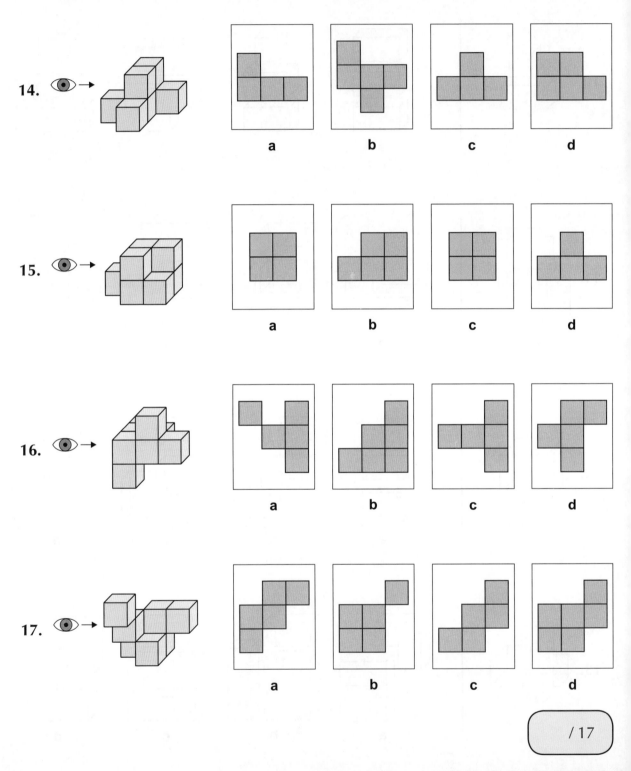

14.

a b c d

15.

a b c d

16.

a b c d

17.

a b c d

/ 17

It's puzzle time! This page will help you practise your **folding** skills.

Creased Shirts

Jerry, Terry and Kerry's shirts are folded up in a large pile of washing.
Match their shirts on the left to the correct shirt in the pile.

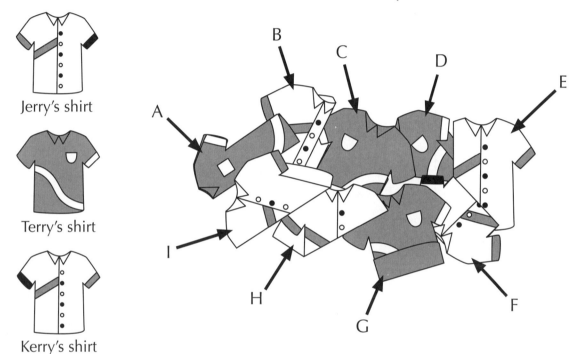

Jerry's shirt

Terry's shirt

Kerry's shirt

Plane Sailing

Sam is following instructions to make a paper aeroplane,
but one of the stages is missing. Draw what the
paper aeroplane would look like at the missing stage.

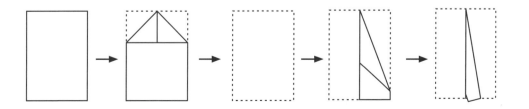

You have **10 minutes** to do this test. Circle the letter for each correct answer.

Work out which option shows the figure on the left when folded along the dotted line.

1.

   a   b   c   d

2.

   a   b   c   d

3.

   a   b   c   d

4.

   a   b   c   d

5.

   a   b   c   d

Work out which of the four cubes can be made from the net.

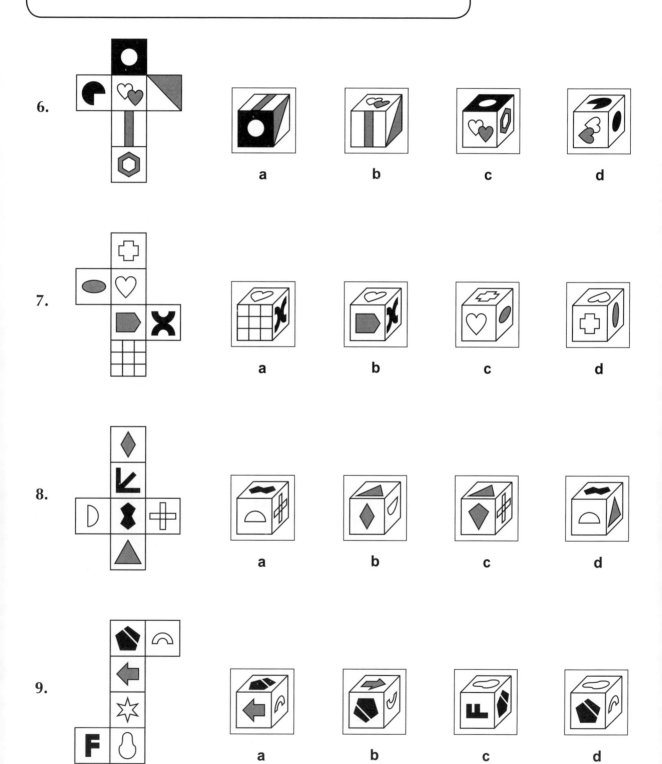

6.

    a   b   c   d

7.

    a   b   c   d

8.

    a   b   c   d

9.

    a   b   c   d

Work out which option can be put together with the figure on the left to make the 3D shape in the grey box.

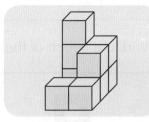

10.

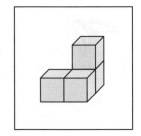

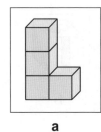
a

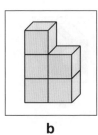
b

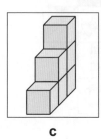
c

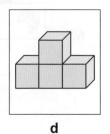
d

11.

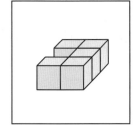

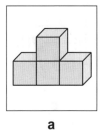
a

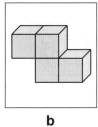
b

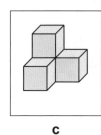
c

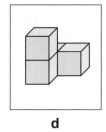
d

12.

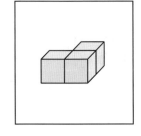

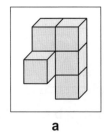
a

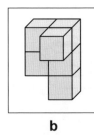
b

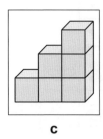
c

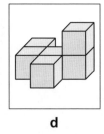
d

13.

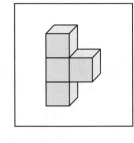

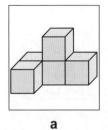
a

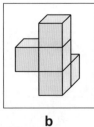
b

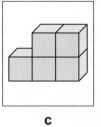
c

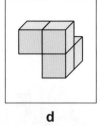
d

Work out which option is the 3D figure viewed from **above**.

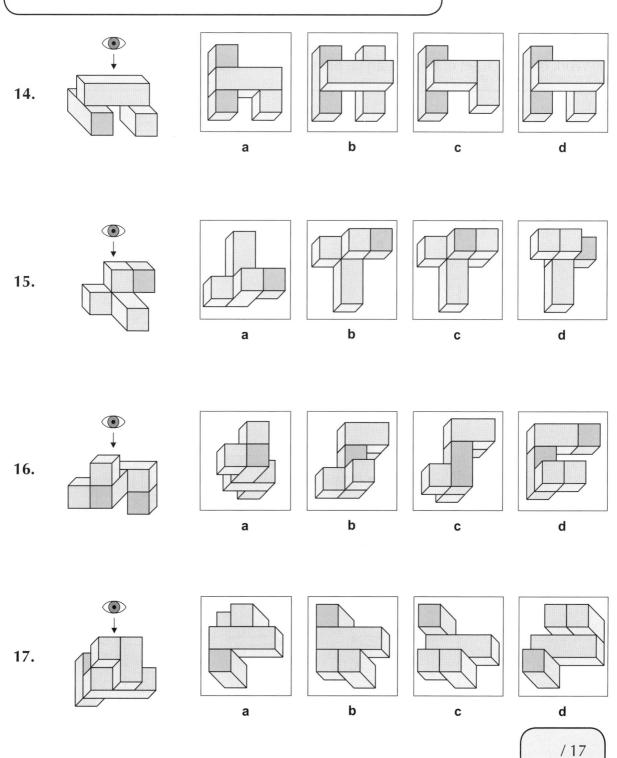

14.

a   b   c   d

15.

a   b   c   d

16.

a   b   c   d

17.

a   b   c   d

/ 17

You have **10 minutes** to do this test. Circle the letter for each correct answer.

Work out which set of blocks can be put together to make the 3D figure on the left.

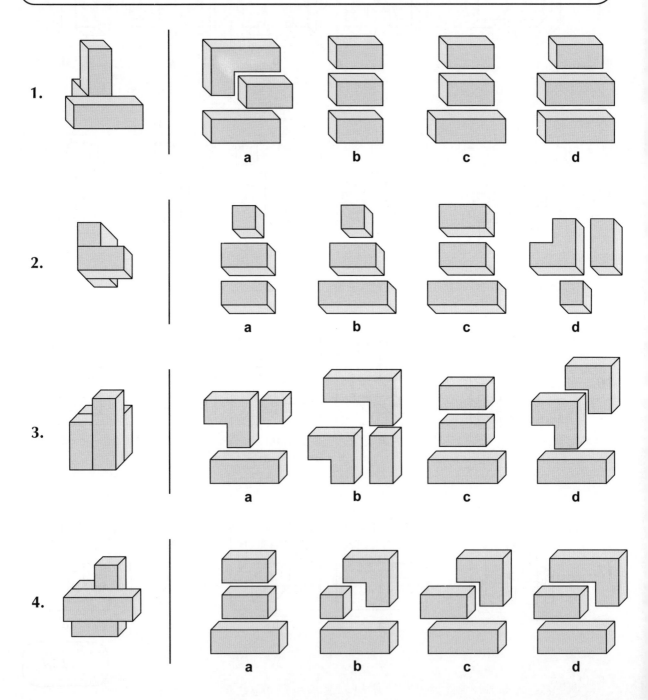

1.

    a   b   c   d

2.

    a   b   c   d

3.

    a   b   c   d

4.

    a   b   c   d

Work out which option shows the figure on the left when folded along the dotted line.

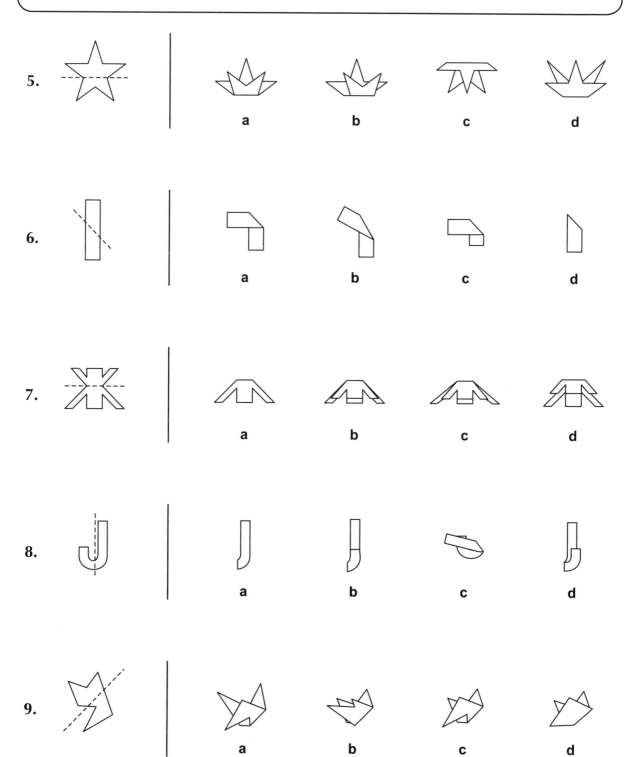

5.

    a   b   c   d

6.

    a   b   c   d

7.

    a   b   c   d

8.

    a   b   c   d

9.

    a   b   c   d

Work out which option is a 2D view from the **right** of the 3D figure shown.

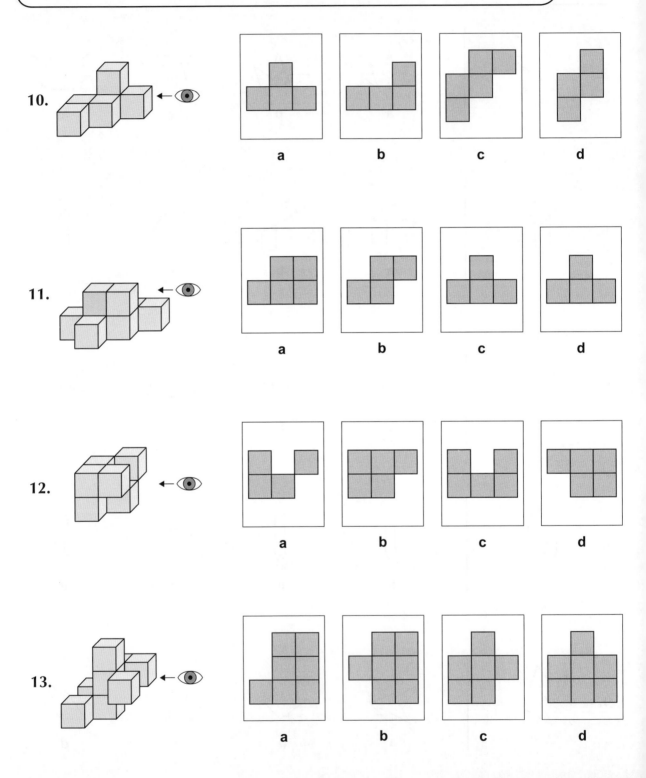

The figures on the left show different views of the same cube. All the cube faces are different. Work out which of the options should replace the blue cube face.

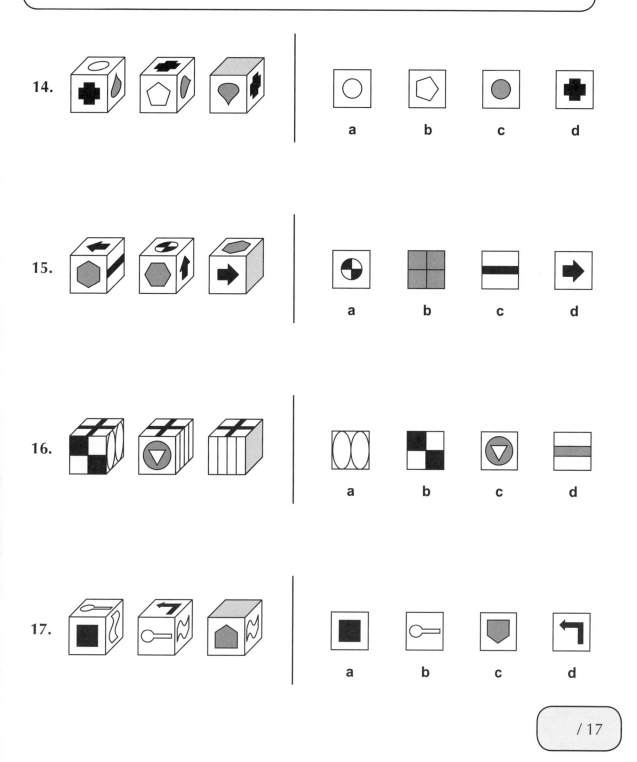

14.

a   b   c   d

15.

a   b   c   d

16.

a   b   c   d

17.

a   b   c   d

/ 17

Test 20

Test 21

You have **10 minutes** to do this test. Circle the letter for each correct answer.

> A square is folded and then a hole is punched, as shown on the left. Work out which option shows the square when unfolded.

1.

     a   b   c   d

2.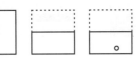

     a   b   c   d

3.

     a   b   c   d

4.

     a   b   c   d

5.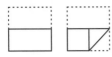

     a   b   c   d

Test 21   94   © CGP — not to be photocopied

Work out which of the 3D shapes can be made from the net.

6.

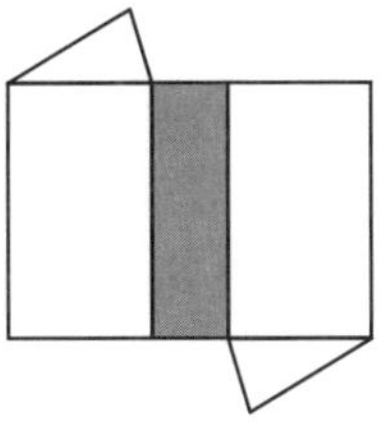

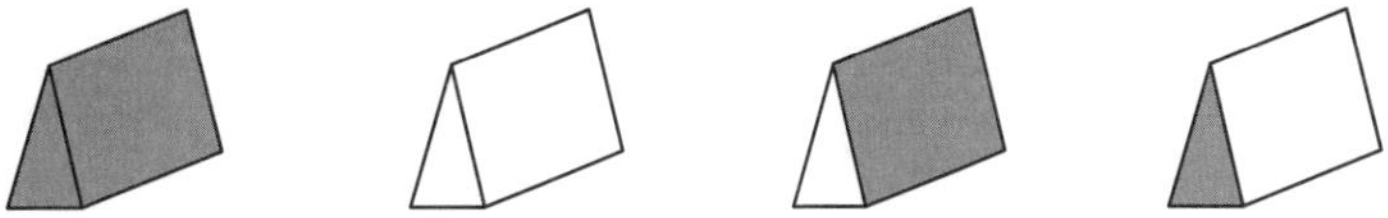

a   b   c   d

7.

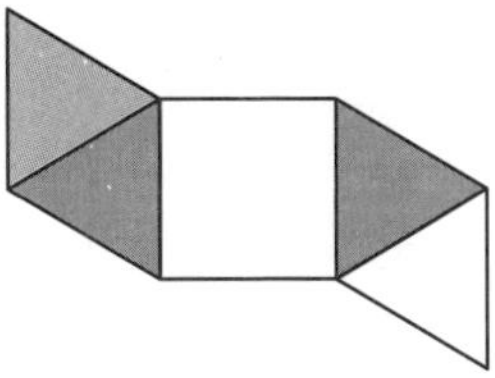

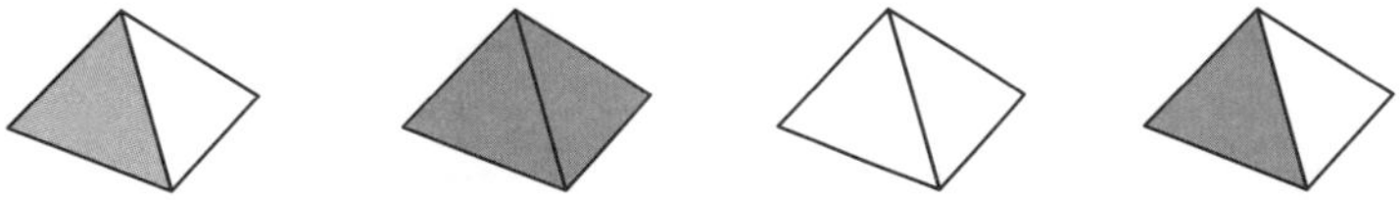

a   b   c   d

8.

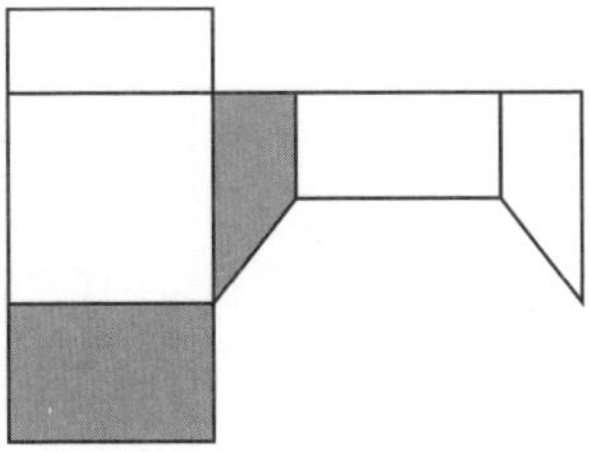

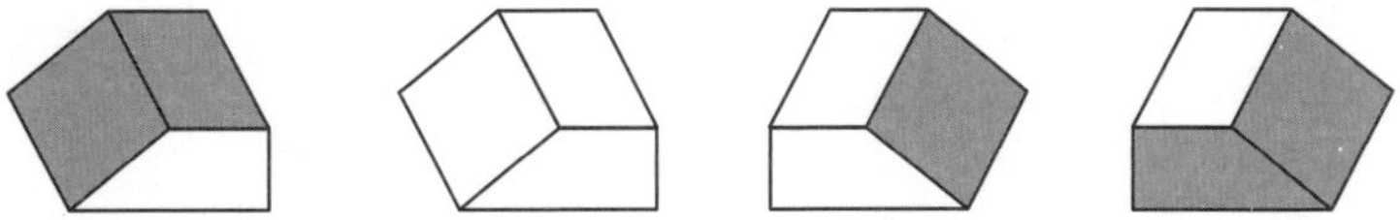

a   b   c   d

9.

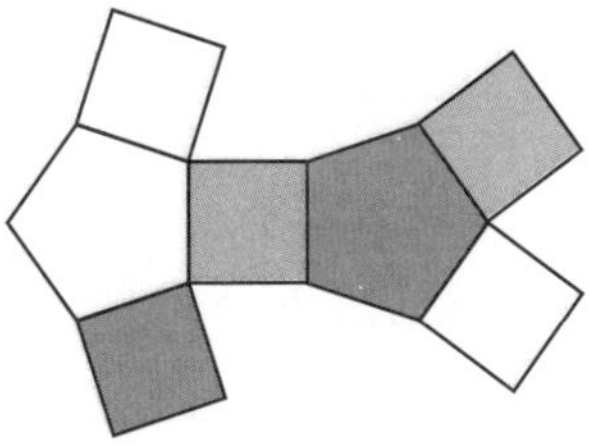

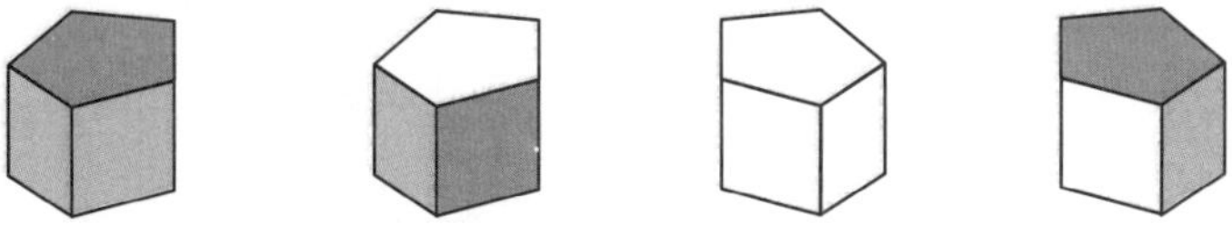

a   b   c   d

Work out which option can be put together with the figure on the left to make the 3D shape in the grey box.

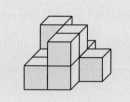

10.

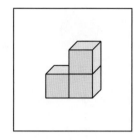   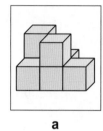   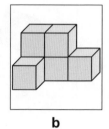   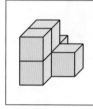   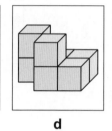

a   b   c   d

11.

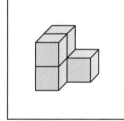   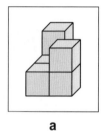   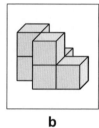   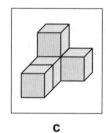   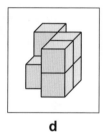

a   b   c   d

12.

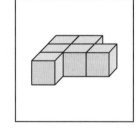   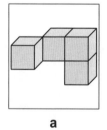   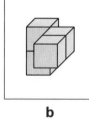   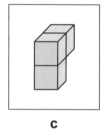   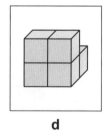

a   b   c   d

13.

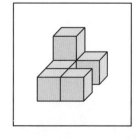   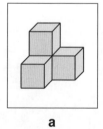   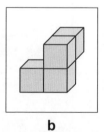   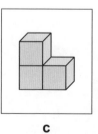   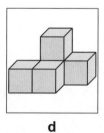

a   b   c   d

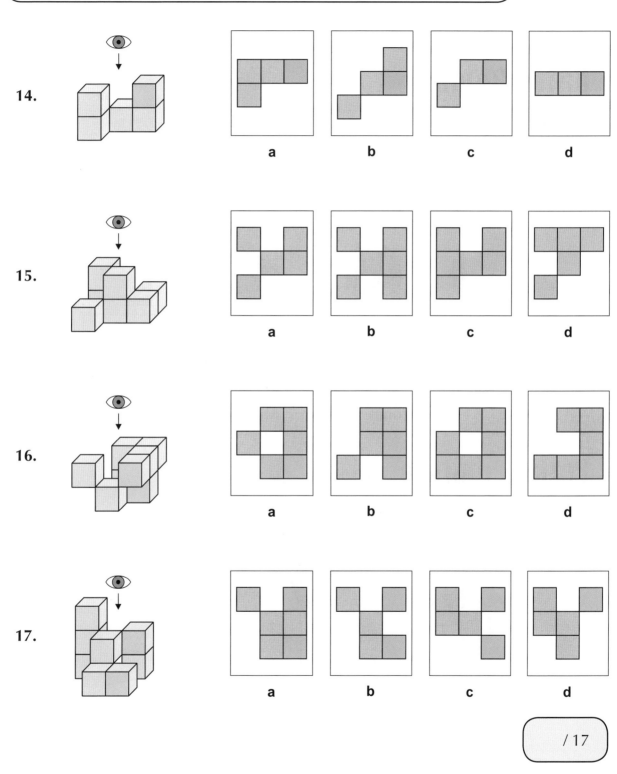

14.

a   b   c   d

15.

a   b   c   d

16.

a   b   c   d

17.

a   b   c   d

/ 17

Time for a couple more puzzles. See if you've got your **block** and **net** skills sorted.

Hairy Heights

The Block Head Gang are trying out a new hat.
The leader of the gang is always the tallest member.
Which member of the gang will be the leader
when they are all wearing the hat?

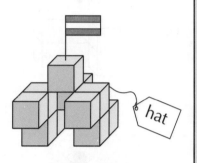

Doug

Jones

Merlin

Trevor

Perky Penguin

Perky can be made by folding a paper net.
Fill in the missing shapes and shadings on Perky's net below.

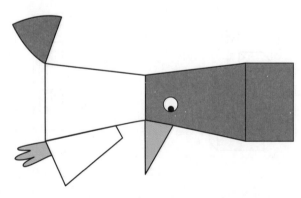

Test 22

You have **10 minutes** to do this test. Circle the letter for each correct answer.

Work out which 3D figure in the grey box has been rotated to make the new 3D figure.

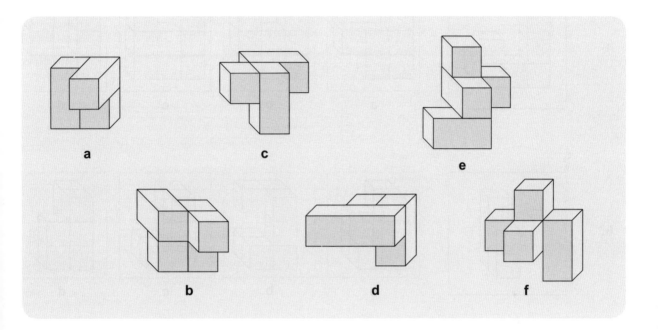

a

c

e

b

d

f

1.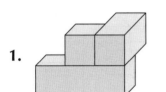

a	d
b	e
c	f

2.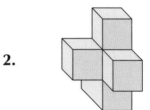

a	d
b	e
c	f

3.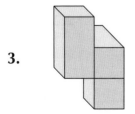

a	d
b	e
c	f

4.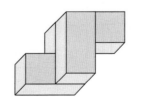

a	d
b	e
c	f

Work out which option can be put together with the figure on the left to make the 3D shape in the grey box.

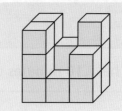

5.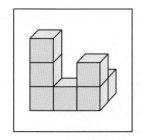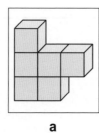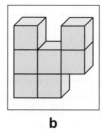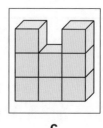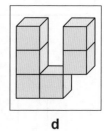

a   b   c   d

6.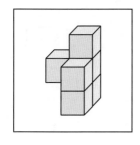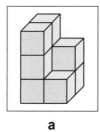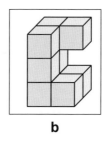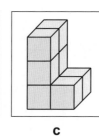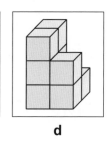

a   b   c   d

7.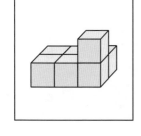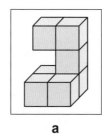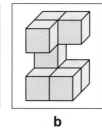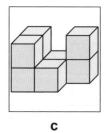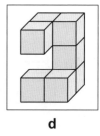

a   b   c   d

8.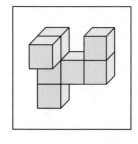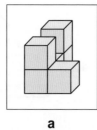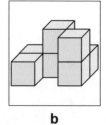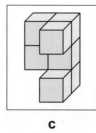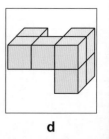

a   b   c   d

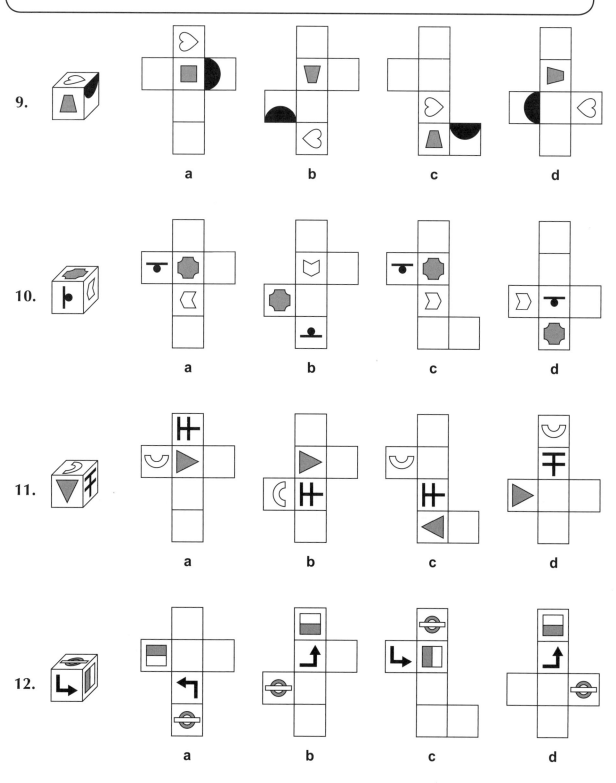

9.

a   b   c   d

10.

a   b   c   d

11.

a   b   c   d

12.

a   b   c   d

Test 22

A square is folded and then a hole is punched, as shown on the left. Work out which option shows the square when unfolded.

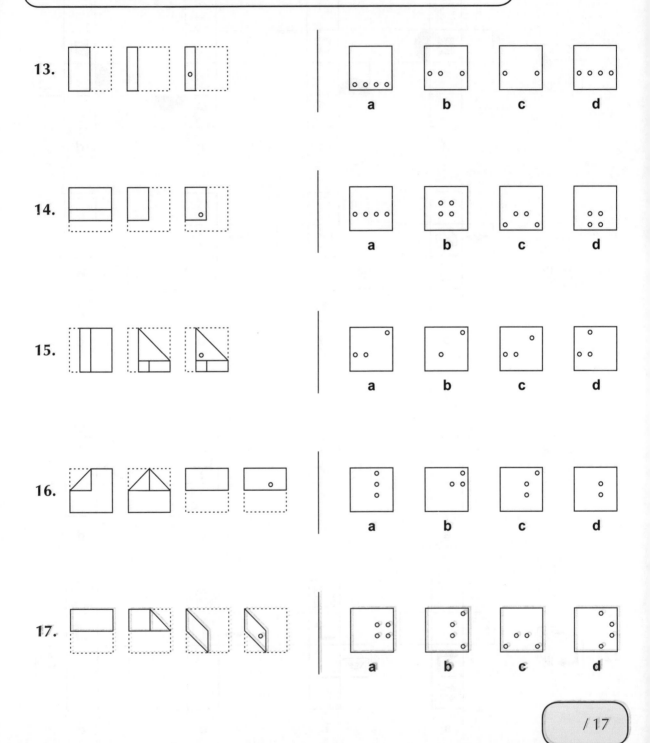

13.
    a   b   c   d

14.
    a   b   c   d

15.
    a   b   c   d

16.
    a   b   c   d

17.
    a   b   c   d

/ 17

102

Test 23

You have **10 minutes** to do this test. Circle the letter for each correct answer.

Work out which set of blocks can be put together to make the 3D figure on the left.

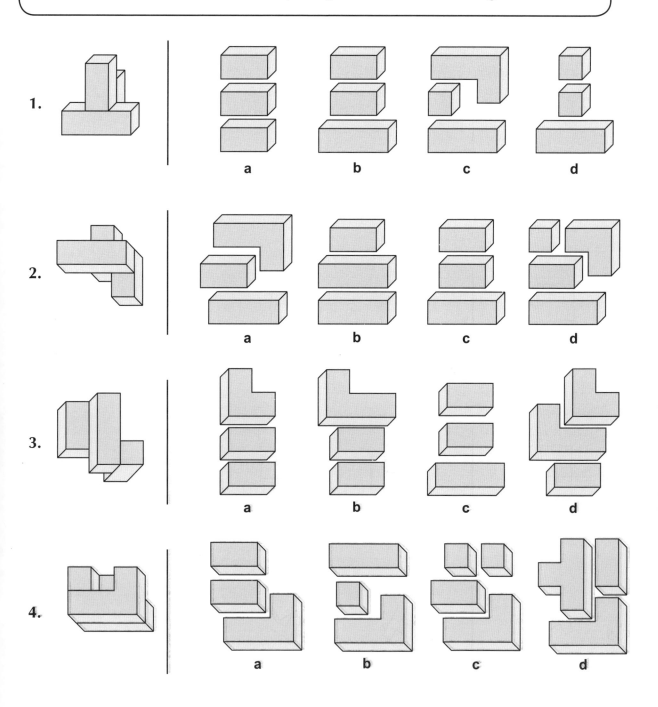

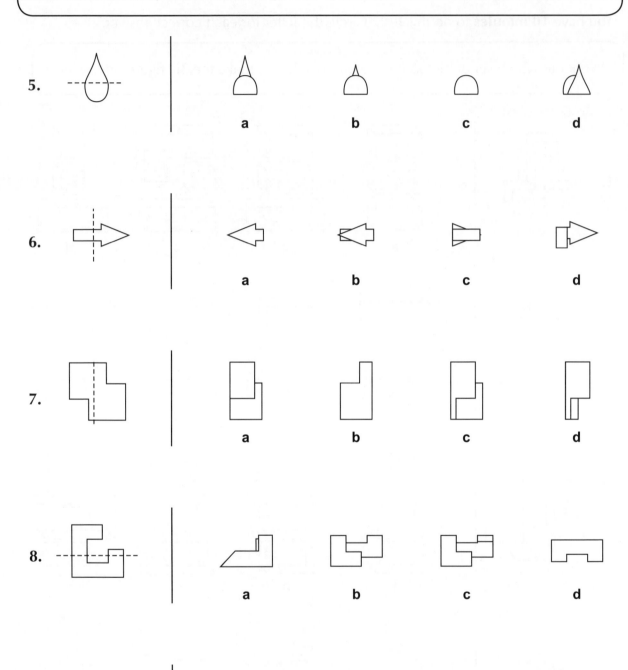

5.

     a   b   c   d

6.

     a   b   c   d

7.

     a   b   c   d

8.

     a   b   c   d

9.

     a   b   c   d

Work out which option is the 3D figure viewed from the **right**.

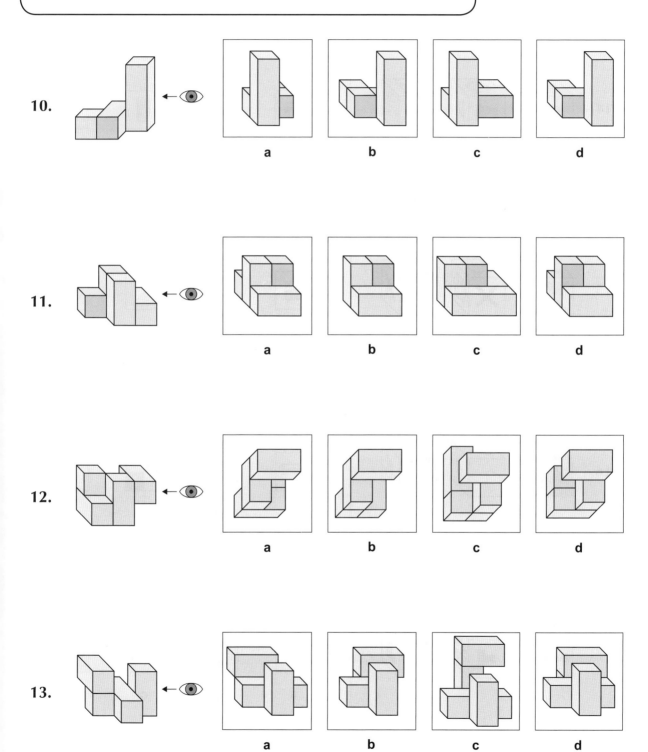

10.

a b c d

11.

a b c d

12.

a b c d

13.

a b c d

The figures on the left show different views of the same cube. All the cube faces are different. Work out which of the options should replace the blue cube face.

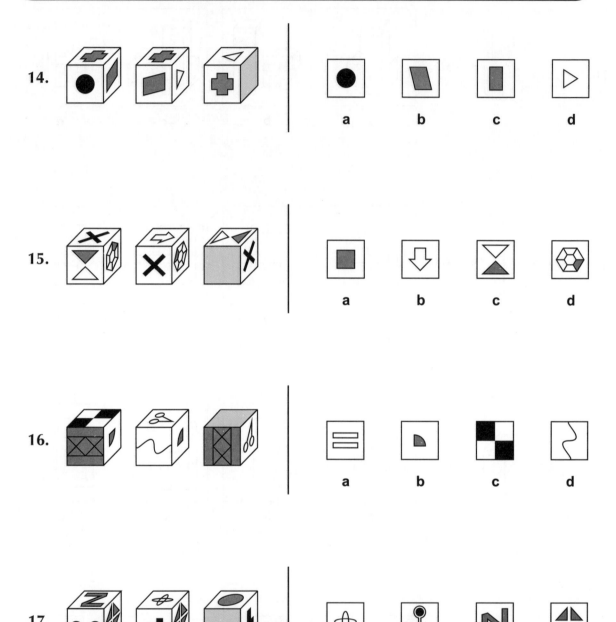

14.

a   b   c   d

15.

a   b   c   d

16.

a   b   c   d

17.

a   b   c   d

/ 17

Test 24

You have **10 minutes** to do this test. Circle the letter for each correct answer.

Work out which option is a 2D view from **above** the 3D figure shown.

1.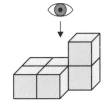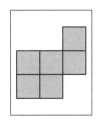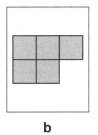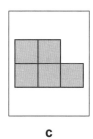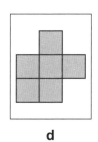

a   b   c   d

2.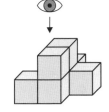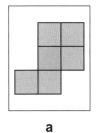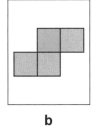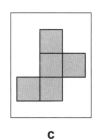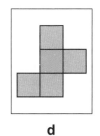

a   b   c   d

3.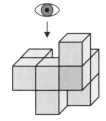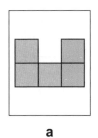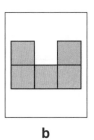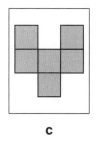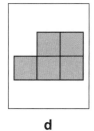

a   b   c   d

4.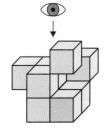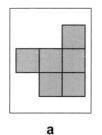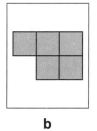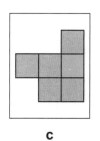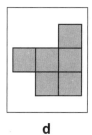

a   b   c   d

Work out which option can be put together with the figure on the left to make the 3D shape in the grey box.

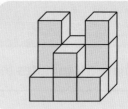

5.

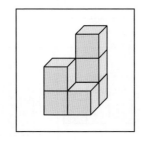

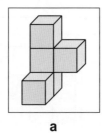

a

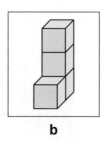

b

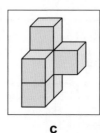

c

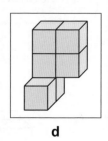

d

6.

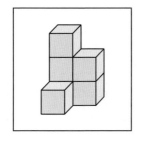

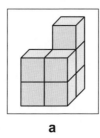

a

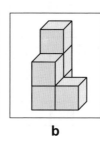

b

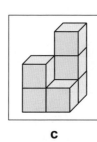

c

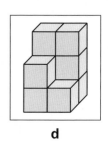

d

7.

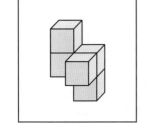

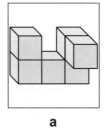

a

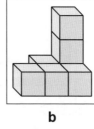

b

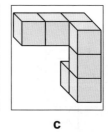

c

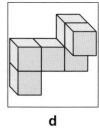

d

8.

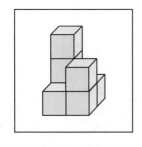

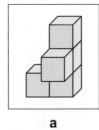

a

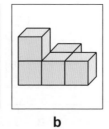

b

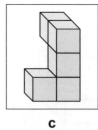

c

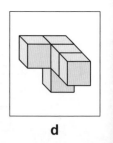

d

Work out which 3D figure in the grey box has been rotated to make the new 3D figure.

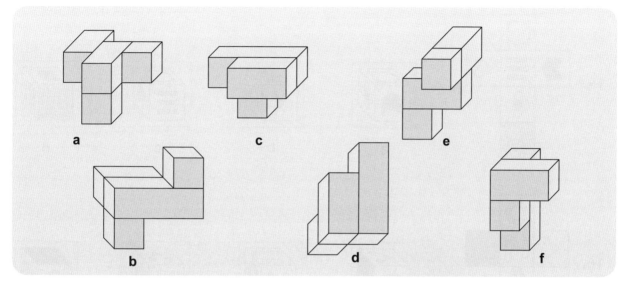

a

c

e

b

d

f

9.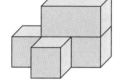

a	d
b	e
c	f

10.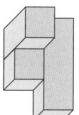

a	d
b	e
c	f

11.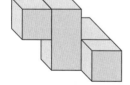

a	d
b	e
c	f

12.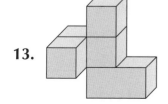

a	d
b	e
c	f

13.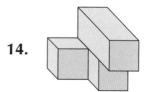

a	d
b	e
c	f

14.

a	d
b	e
c	f

109

Work out which of the four cubes can be made from the net.

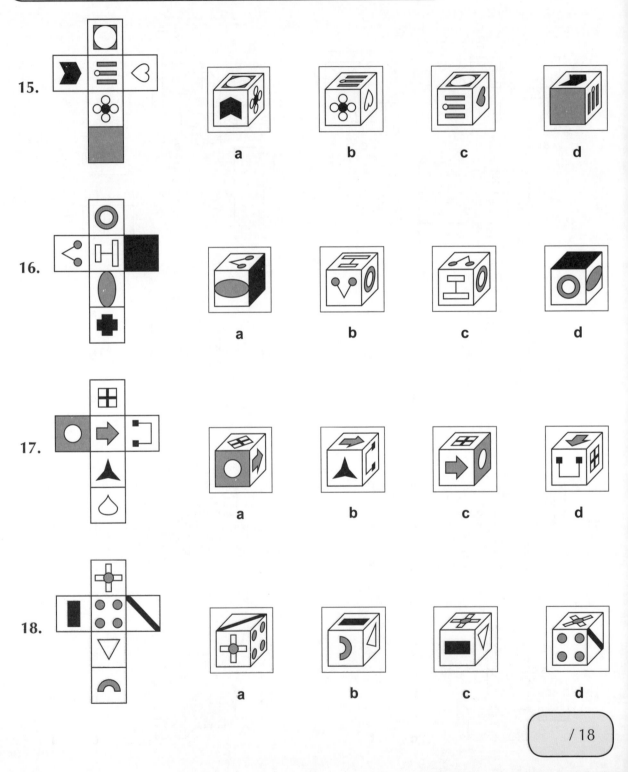

15.   a   b   c   d

16.   a   b   c   d

17.   a   b   c   d

18.   a   b   c   d

/ 18

Time for a break. These puzzles will help you practise your **rotation** and **net** skills.

Block Cat

Holly has made four cats out of blocks. Three of the cats are identical and one has been built slightly differently. Circle the odd one out.

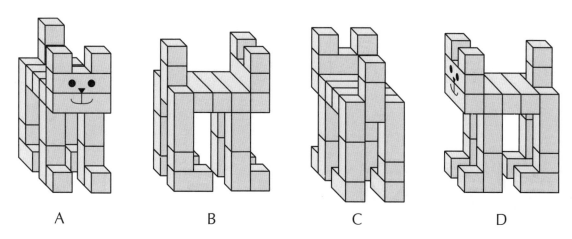

A   B   C   D

Cube Chaos

The cube nets below are missing numbers and dots from some of their faces. Each net folds to make the cube next to it. The cube shows the faces that the net is missing. Faces that are opposite each other have dots of the same colour. Use the cubes to fill in the missing numbers and dots on the nets.

1.   2.

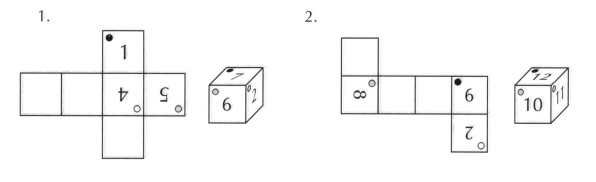

You have **10 minutes** to do this test. Circle the letter for each correct answer.

> The figures on the left show different views of the same cube. All the cube faces are different. Work out which of the options should replace the blue cube face.

1.

        a   b   c   d

2.

        a   b   c   d

3.

        a   b   c   d

4.

        a   b   c   d

Work out which of the 3D shapes can be made from the net.

5.

a   b   c   d

6.

a   b   c   d

7.

a   b   c   d

8.

a   b   c   d

Test 25

A square is folded and then a hole is punched, as shown on the left. Work out which option shows the square when unfolded.

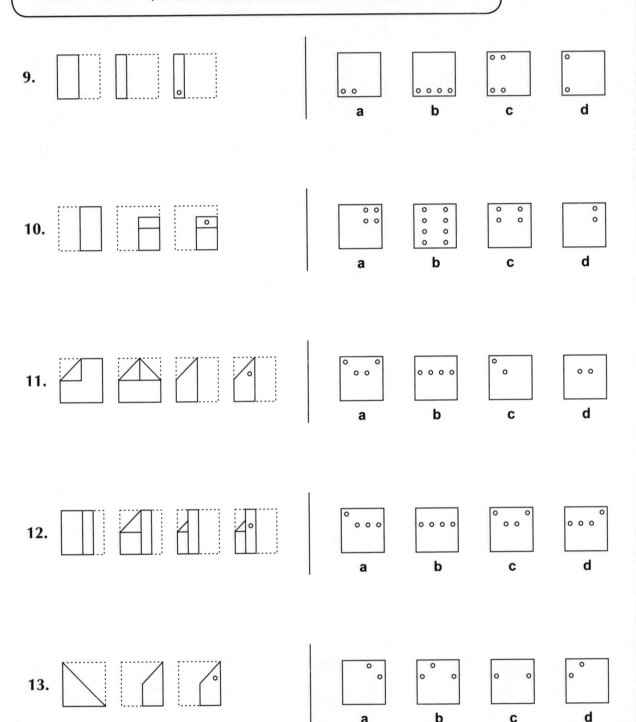

9.

           a   b   c   d

10.

           a   b   c   d

11.

           a   b   c   d

12.

           a   b   c   d

13.

           a   b   c   d

Work out which option can be put together with the
figure on the left to make the 3D shape in the grey box.

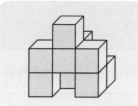

14.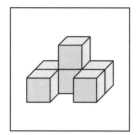

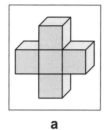
a

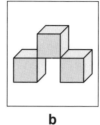
b

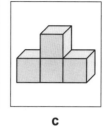
c

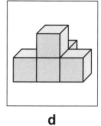
d

15.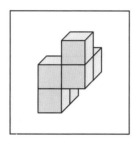

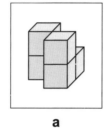
a

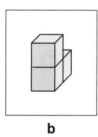
b

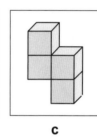
c

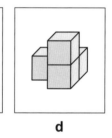
d

16.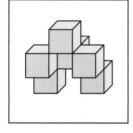

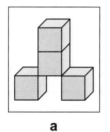
a

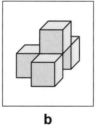
b

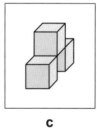
c

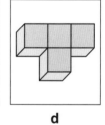
d

17.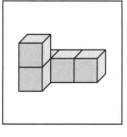

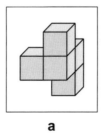
a

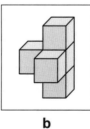
b

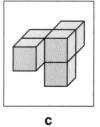
c

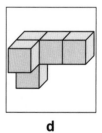
d

/ 17

Test 25

You have **10 minutes** to do this test. Circle the letter for each correct answer.

Work out which option is a 2D view from the **back** of the 3D figure shown.

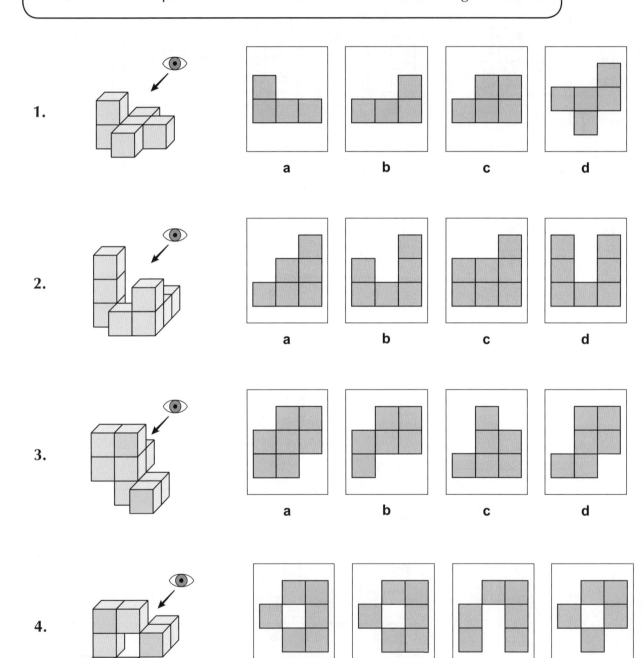

1.

    a   b   c   d

2.

    a   b   c   d

3.

    a   b   c   d

4.

    a   b   c   d

116

Work out which of the four cubes can be made from the net.

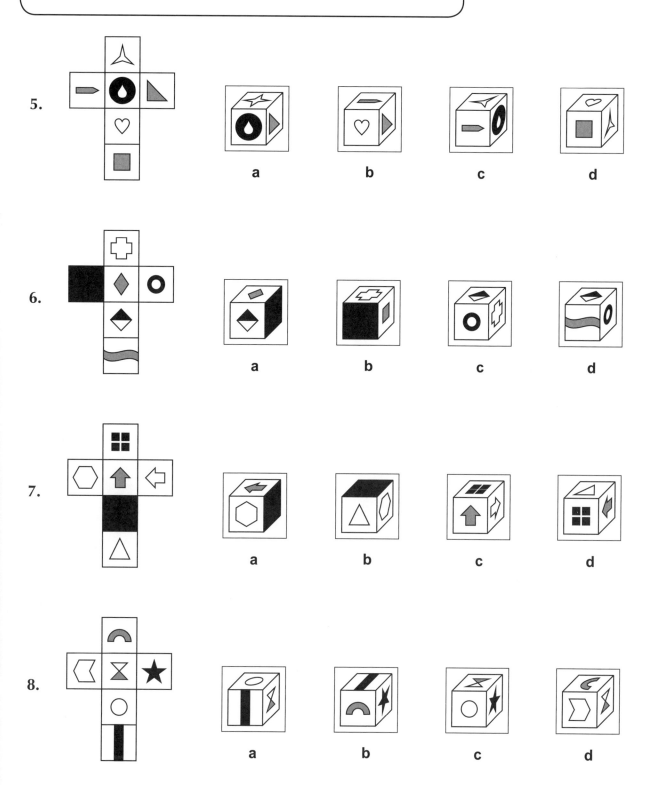

5.

a   b   c   d

6.

a   b   c   d

7.

a   b   c   d

8.

a   b   c   d

9.

a   b   c   d

10.

a   b   c   d

11.

a   b   c   d

12.

a   b   c   d

13. 

a   b   c   d

Work out which set of blocks can be put together to make the 3D figure on the left.

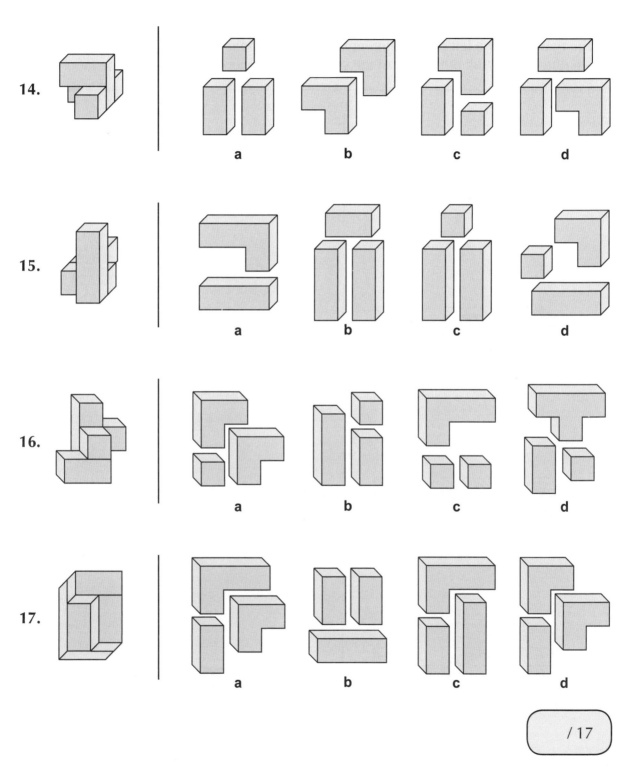

14.   a   b   c   d

15.   a   b   c   d

16.   a   b   c   d

17.   a   b   c   d

/ 17

Test 26

Test 27

You have **10 minutes** to do this test. Circle the letter for each correct answer.

The figures on the left show different views of the same cube. All the cube faces are different. Work out which of the options should replace the blue cube face.

1.

                                             a   b   c   d

2.

                                             a   b   c   d

3.

                                             a   b   c   d

4.

                                             a   b   c   d

   120

Work out which 3D figure in the grey box has been rotated to make the new 3D figure.

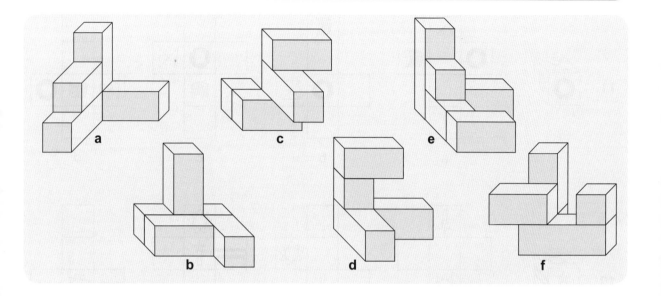

5.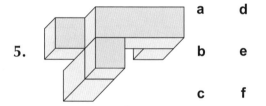

a   d

b   e

c   f

6.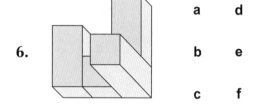

a   d

b   e

c   f

7.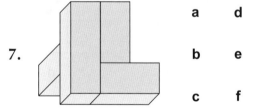

a   d

b   e

c   f

8.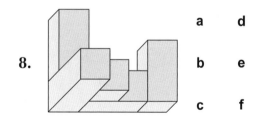

a   d

b   e

c   f

9.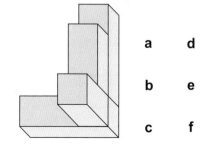

a   d

b   e

c   f

10.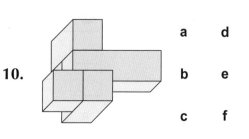

a   d

b   e

c   f

Test 27

Work out which of the four partial nets can be folded to make the cube on the left.

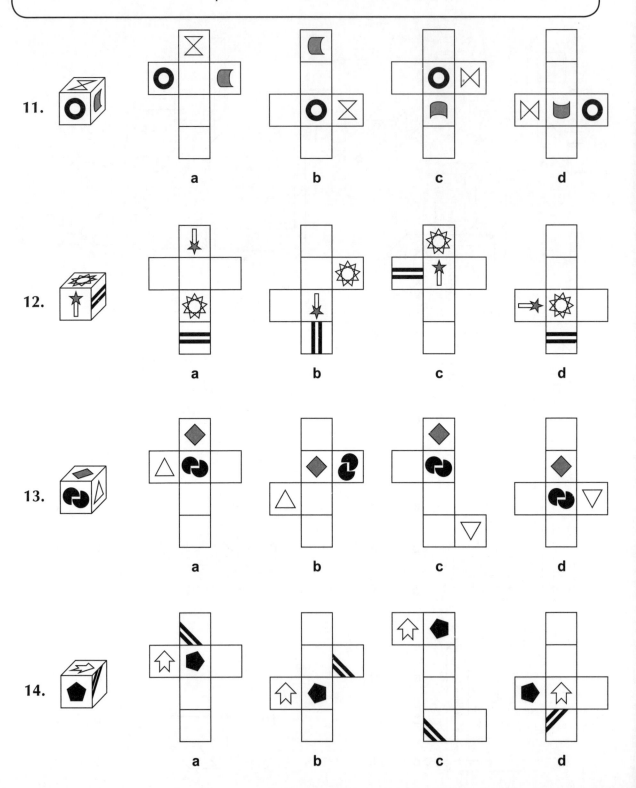

11.

a b c d

12.

a b c d

13.

a b c d

14.

a b c d

Work out which option is a 2D view from the **right** of the 3D figure shown.

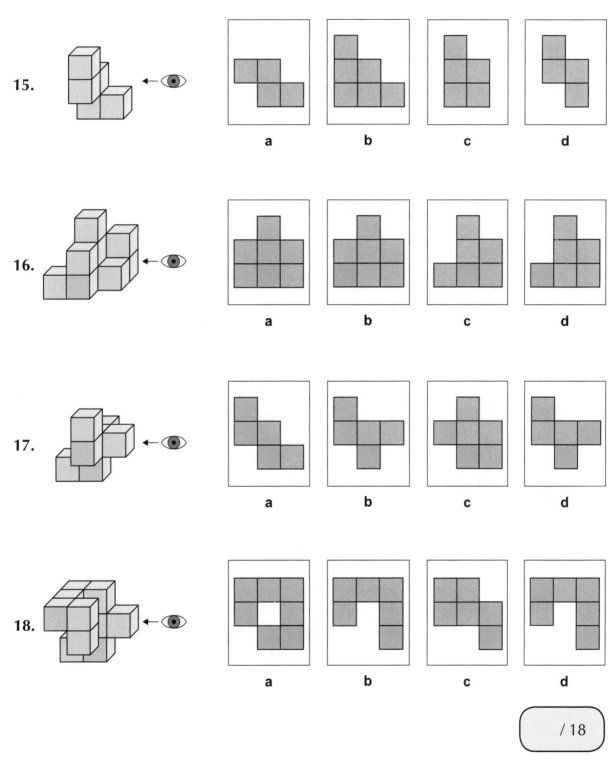

15.

a b c d

16.

a b c d

17.

a b c d

18.

a b c d

/ 18

123

Try these puzzles to help you practise your skills with **building blocks** and **cube views**.

Witch Door?

Claire bumps into an evil witch who threatens to turn her into stone if she can't solve a puzzle. One of the doors below will lead Claire to safety. She has to choose the door with the shape in front of it which can be made from all the blocks on the right. Which door should Claire choose?

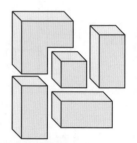

A   **B**   **C**   **D**

Cube Confusion

Joss has six identical cubes. He arranges the cubes in order from left to right so that the number of sides of the shape on the front face goes up by one. Draw the missing faces of the last three cubes in the empty squares below.

124

You have **10 minutes** to do this test. Circle the letter for each correct answer.

Work out which option shows the figure on the left when folded along the dotted line.

1.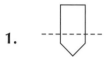

        a   b   c   d

2.

        a   b   c   d

3.

        a   b   c   d

4.

        a   b   c   d

5.

        a   b   c   d

Test 28

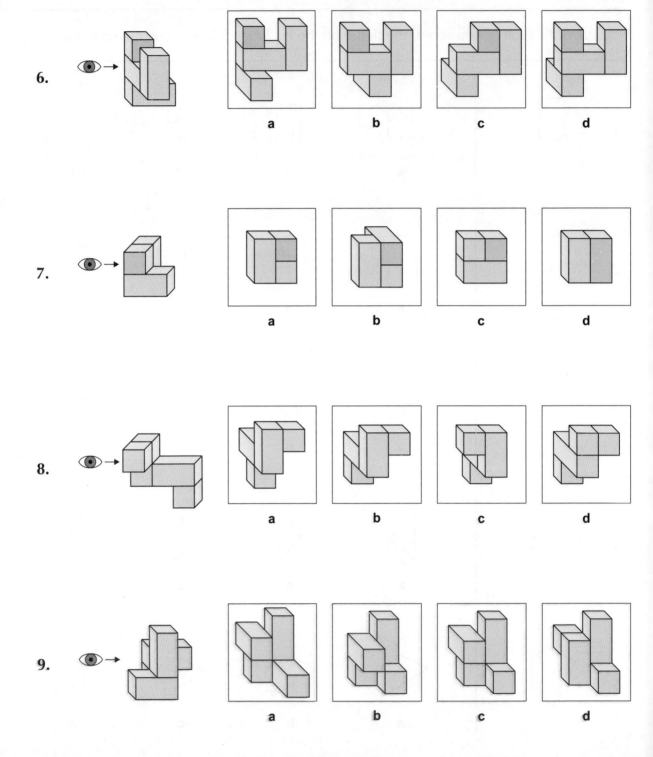

6.

a b c d

7.

a b c d

8.

a b c d

9.

a b c d

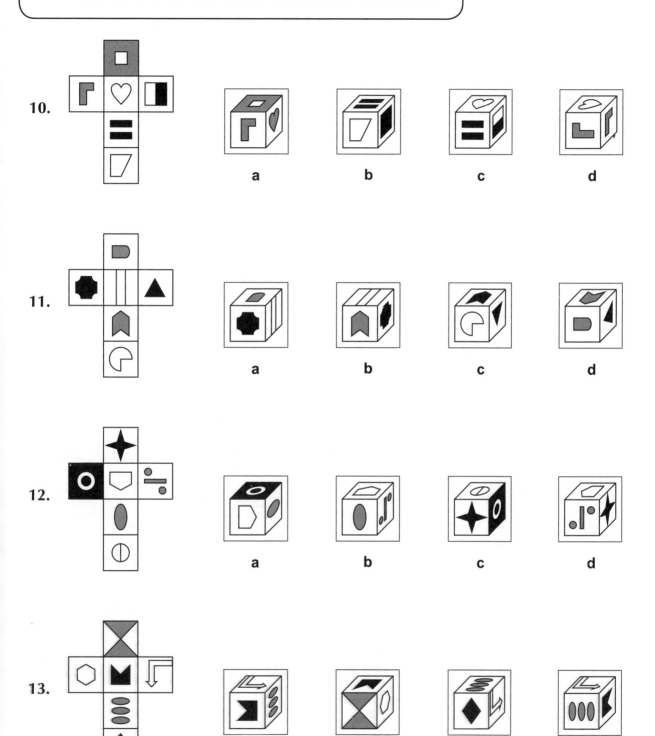

10.

a　　b　　c　　d

11.

a　　b　　c　　d

12.

a　　b　　c　　d

13.

a　　b　　c　　d

Work out which option can be put together with the figure on the left to make the 3D shape in the grey box.

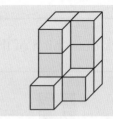

14.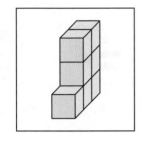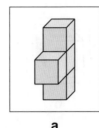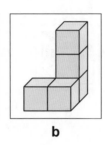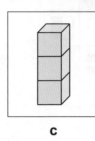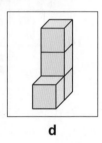

a b c d

15.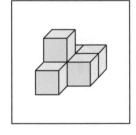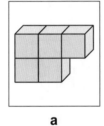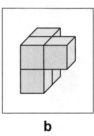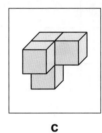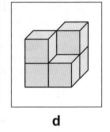

a b c d

16.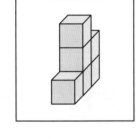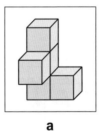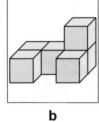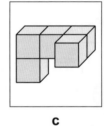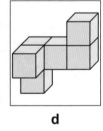

a b c d

17.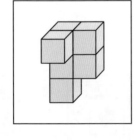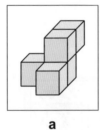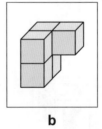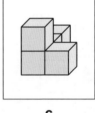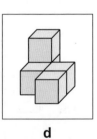

a b c d

/ 17

Test 29

You have **10 minutes** to do this test. Circle the letter for each correct answer.

Work out which option is a 2D view from the **right** of the 3D figure shown.

1.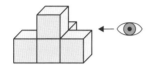

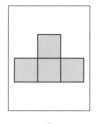   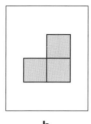   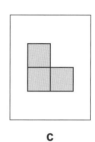   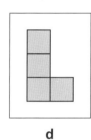

        a   b   c   d

2.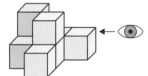

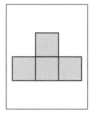   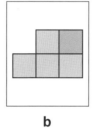   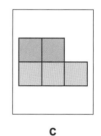   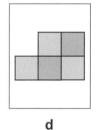

        a   b   c   d

3.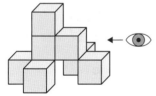

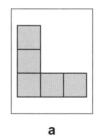   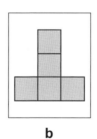   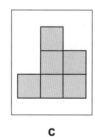   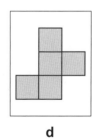

        a   b   c   d

4.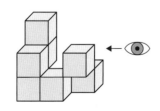

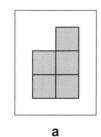   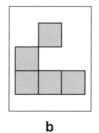   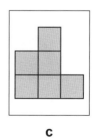   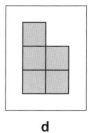

        a   b   c   d

© CGP — not to be photocopied   129   Test 29

Work out which of the 3D shapes can be made from the net.

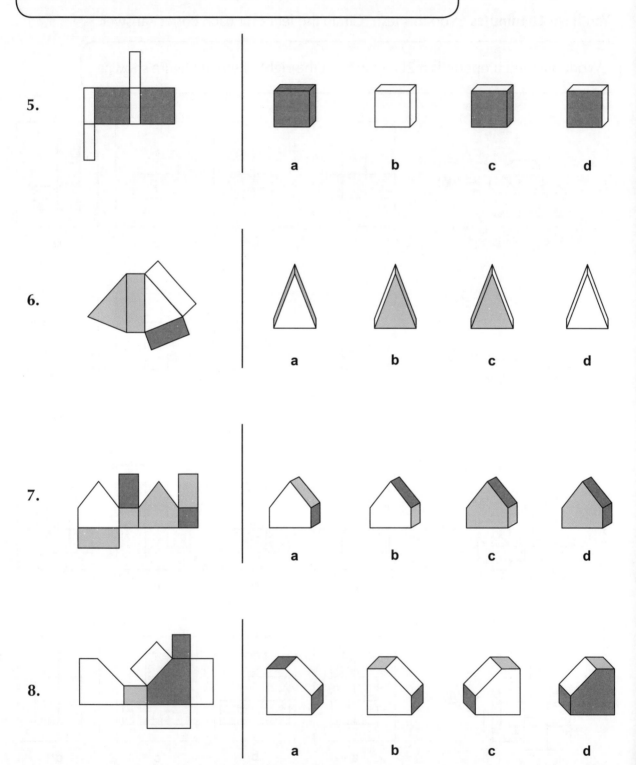

5.

a b c d

6.

a b c d

7.

a b c d

8.

a b c d

130

Work out which 3D figure in the grey box has been rotated to make the new 3D figure.

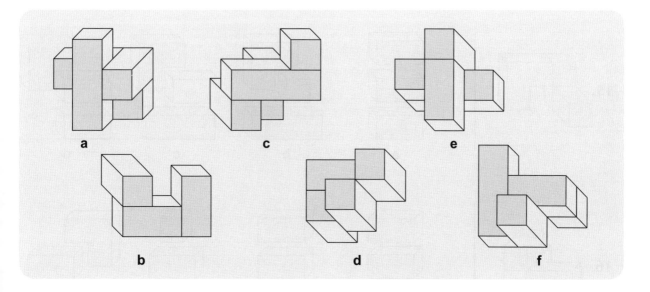

a

c

e

b

d

f

9.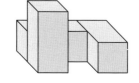

a   d

b   e

c   f

10.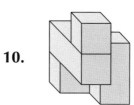

a   d

b   e

c   f

11.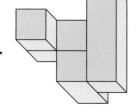

a   d

b   e

c   f

12.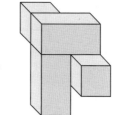

a   d

b   e

c   f

13.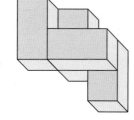

a   d

b   e

c   f

14.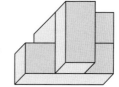

a   d

b   e

c   f

Work out which set of blocks can be put together to make the 3D figure on the left.

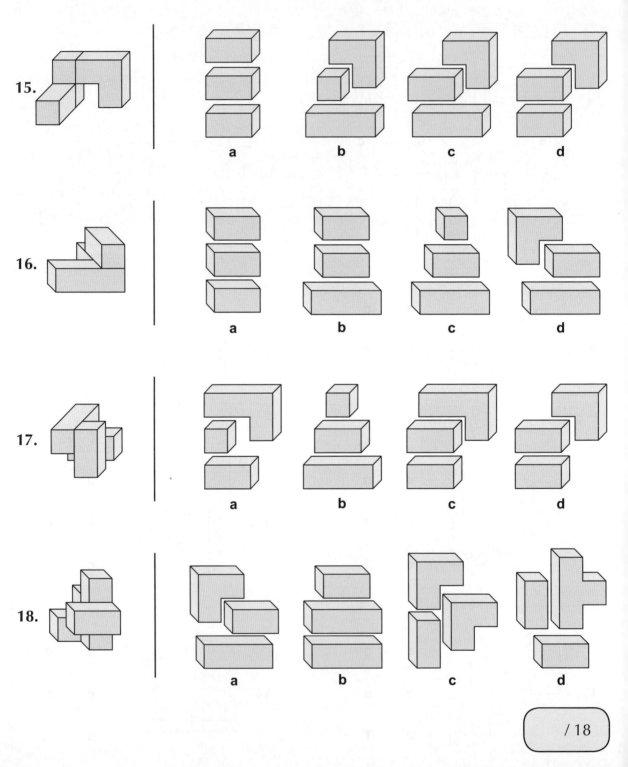

15.

a   b   c   d

16.

a   b   c   d

17.

a   b   c   d

18.

a   b   c   d

/ 18

Test 30

You have **10 minutes** to do this test. Circle the letter for each correct answer.

> Work out which option is a 2D view from **above** the 3D figure shown.

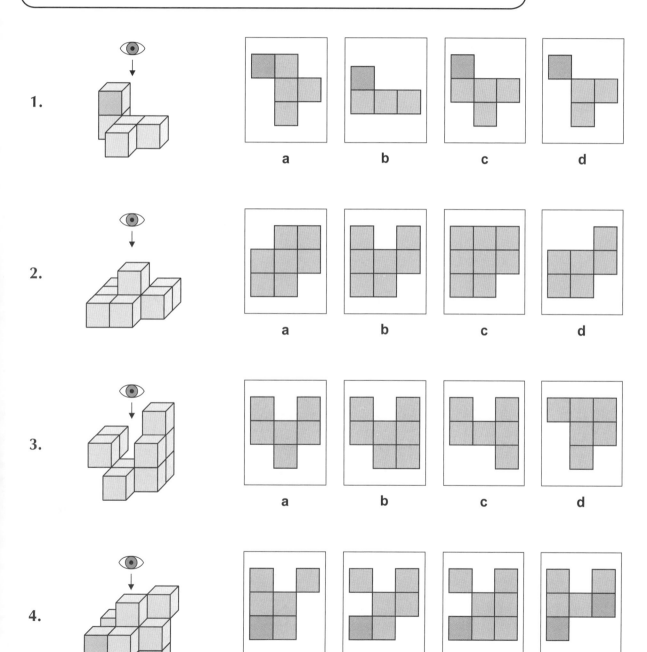

1.

 a b c d

2.

 a b c d

3.

 a b c d

4.

 a b c d

133

Work out which option shows the figure on the left when folded along the dotted line.

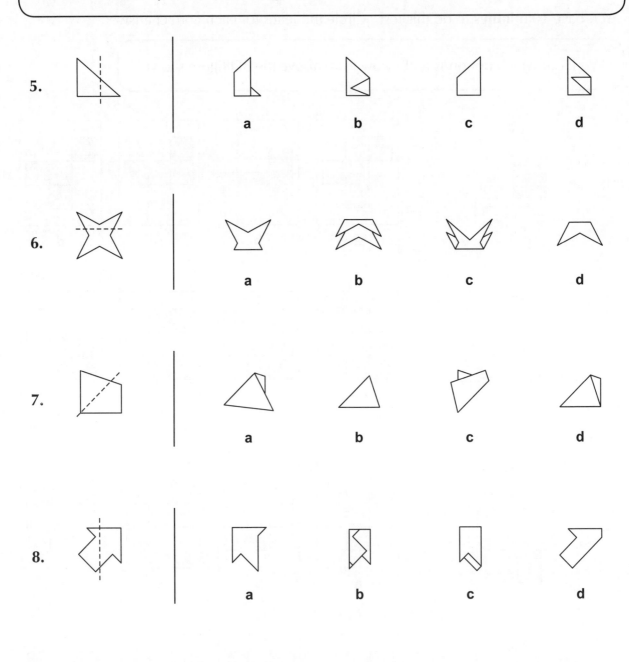

5.

    a   b   c   d

6.

    a   b   c   d

7.

    a   b   c   d

8.

    a   b   c   d

9.

    a   b   c   d

Work out which of the four partial nets can be folded to make the cube on the left.

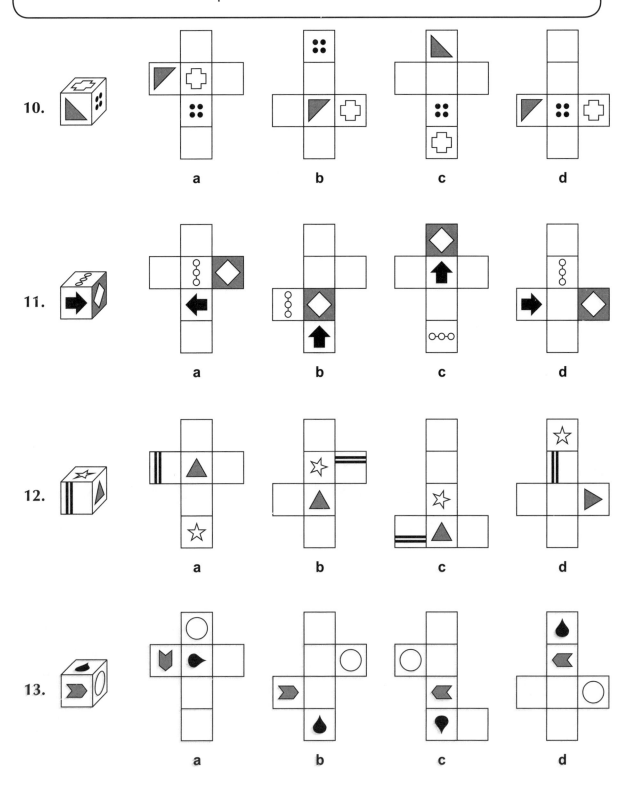

10.

a   b   c   d

11.

a   b   c   d

12.

a   b   c   d

13.

a   b   c   d

135

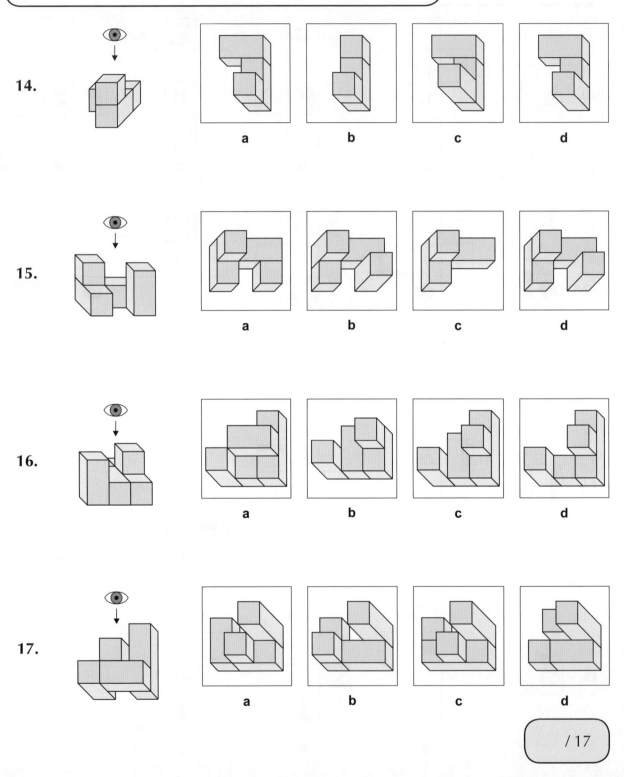

14.

a   b   c   d

15.

a   b   c   d

16.

a   b   c   d

17.

a   b   c   d

/ 17

You have **10 minutes** to do this test. Circle the letter for each correct answer.

Work out which 3D figure in the grey box has been rotated to make the new 3D figure.

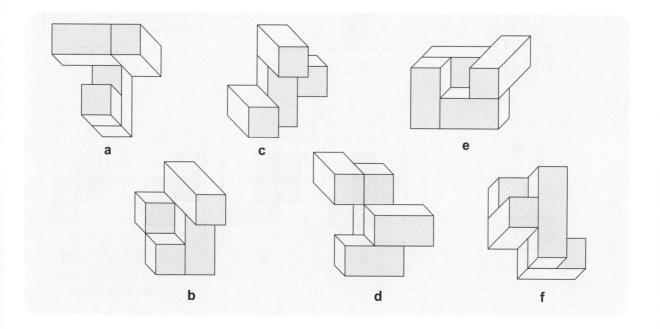

a   c   e

b   d   f

1.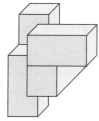

a   d

b   e

c   f

2.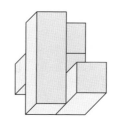

a   d

b   e

c   f

3.

a   d

b   e

c   f

4.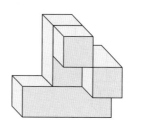

a   d

b   e

c   f

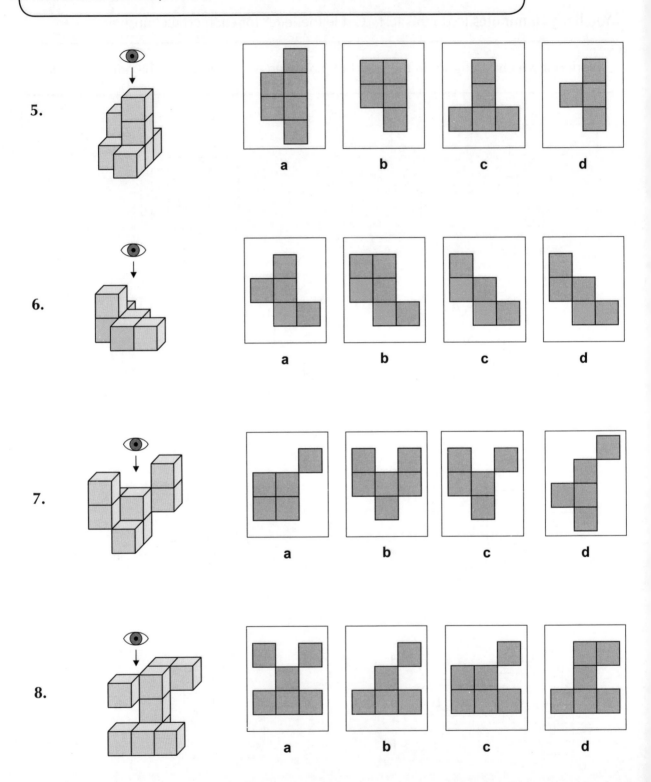

5.

a   b   c   d

6.

a   b   c   d

7.

a   b   c   d

8.

a   b   c   d

Work out which of the four cubes can be made from the net.

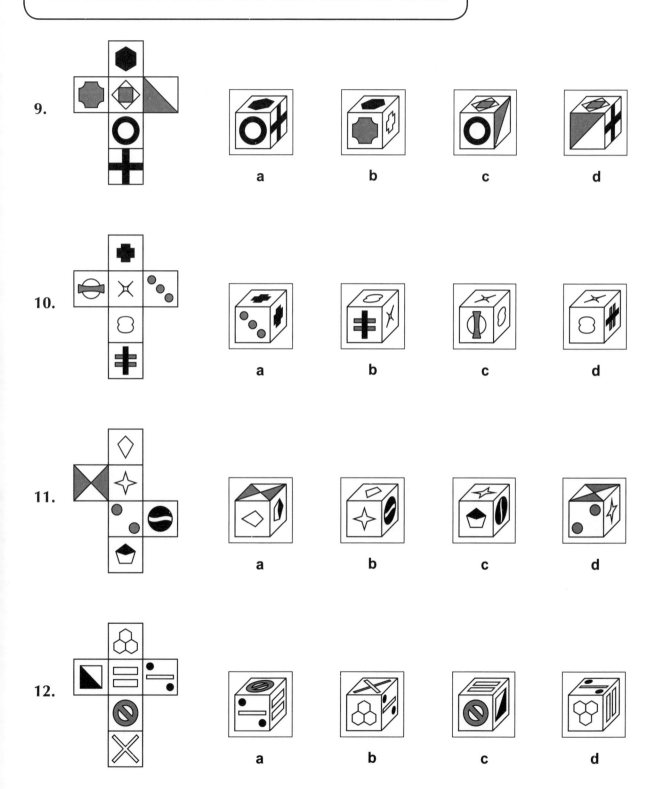

9.

a   b   c   d

10.

a   b   c   d

11.

a   b   c   d

12.

a   b   c   d

Test 31

Work out which option shows the figure on the left when folded along the dotted line.

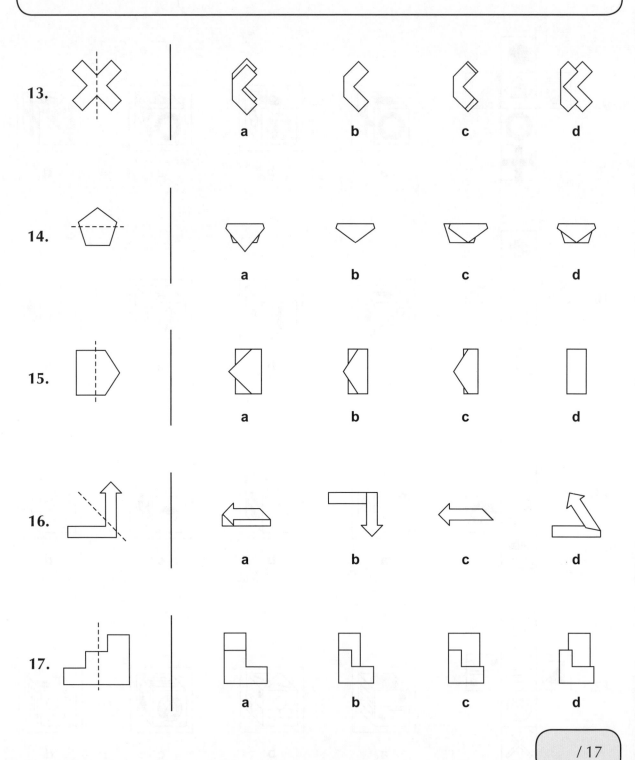

13.

a   b   c   d

14.

a   b   c   d

15.

a   b   c   d

16.

a   b   c   d

17.

a   b   c   d

/ 17

Phew. That's all the tests done. Now for a final bit of fun practice.

Geometric Gerald

Gerald the Geometric Gerbil has nibbled away the corners of a box.
One possible net of the box is shown below on the right.

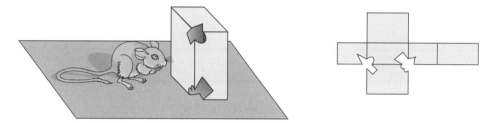

Decide which <u>two</u> of the options below are also nets of the nibbled box.

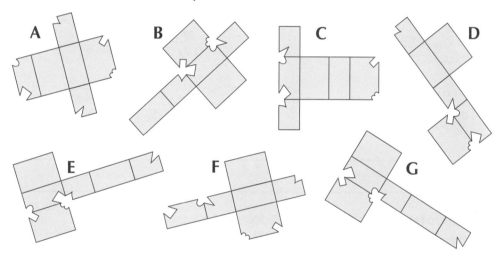

A   B   C   D

E   F   G

Next, Gerald nibbles a 'G' in a neatly folded square tablecloth.
Draw how the holes would appear as the tablecloth is unfolded.

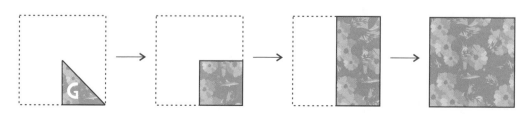

Glossary

Folding Nets

Nets should be folded **into the page**.

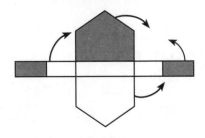

Fold the faces away from you until they all come together.

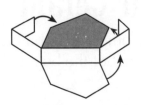

This shape can now be rotated.

3D Rotation

There are **three planes** that a 3D shape can be rotated in.

1. 90 degrees towards you, top-to-bottom

90 degrees away from you, top-to-bottom

2. 90 degrees left-to-right

90 degrees right-to-left

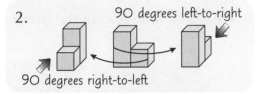

3. 90 degrees anticlockwise in the plane of the page

90 degrees clockwise in the plane of the page

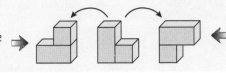

Cubes and Nets

Cubes can be **rotated** in different directions.
Start with the cube view shown on the **left**.

2
4	1	3
5
6

Turning 180 degrees...

... left-to-right gives:

... top-to-bottom gives:

... in the plane of the page gives:

Turning 90 degrees...

... left-to-right gives:

... towards you, top-to-bottom gives:

... anticlockwise in the plane of the page gives:

11+

3D & Spatial

Ages 10-11

The 10-Minute Tests Answer Book

Book 2

Non-Verbal Reasoning
3D & Spatial

Practise • Prepare • Pass

Everything your child needs for 11+ success

Test 1 — pages 8-11

1. B
Shape B has been rotated 90 degrees towards you, top-to-bottom. It has then been rotated 180 degrees in the plane of the page.

2. E
Shape E has been rotated 90 degrees right-to-left.

3. D
Shape D has been rotated 90 degrees towards you, top-to-bottom.

4. A
Shape A has been rotated 180 degrees towards you, top-to-bottom.

5. C
Option A is ruled out because the triangle and the grey star must be on opposite sides. Option B is ruled out because there is no black rectangle. Option D is ruled out because the triangle and the grey star must be on opposite sides.

6. D
Option A is ruled out because the straight sides of the grey arch should be closest to the droplets. Option B is ruled out because the cross and the L shape must be on opposite sides. Option C is ruled out because if the grey face is at the front and the droplets are on the top, then the L shape should be on the right.

7. A
Option B is ruled out because the white arrow should point towards the overlapping ovals. Option C is ruled out because the grey arrow and the black oval must be on opposite sides. Option D is ruled out because if the white arrow is at the front and the overlapping ovals are on the top, then the grey arrow should be on the right.

8. C
Option A is ruled out because if the hexagon is at the front and the grey square is on the top, then the black stripe should be on the right. Option B is ruled out because if the grey square is at the front and the hexagon is on the top, then the spiral should be on the right. Option D is ruled out because the triangle should point away from the black stripe.

9. A
There are three blocks visible from the left, which rules out options C and D. There are two blocks visible on the left, which rules out option B.

10. C
There are three blocks visible along the bottom, which rules out option D. There are two blocks visible on the left, which rules out options A and B.

11. B
There is a blue block visible at the top right. This rules out options A and C. There is a grey block visible at the bottom right. This rules out option D.

12. C
There are two blue blocks visible at the bottom. This rules out options B and D. There are two grey blocks visible at the top. This rules out option A.

13. B

14. A
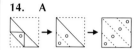

15. B
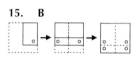

16. D
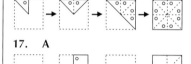

17. A

Test 2 — pages 12-15

1. B
There should only be a block two cubes high in the closest layer when viewed from above, which rules out option A. There should be two cubes at the back, which rules out options C and D.

2. D
There should only be one cube in the closest layer when viewed from above, which rules out options A and B. There should be one cube behind another cube on the left, which rules out option C.

3. C
There should be a block two cubes high on the left, which rules out option A. There should be a block two cubes long at the front right on the bottom, which rules out option B. There should be a grey cube at the back, which rules out option D.

4. B
There should be a cube on the right in the closest layer when viewed from above, which rules out option A. There should be one cube on the left of the figure, which rules out options C and D.

5. A
Option B is ruled out because there is no solid grey circle on the cube. Option C is ruled out because the white curved shape and the grey ring are on opposite sides. Option D is ruled out because the black cross and the grey ring are on opposite sides.

6. B
Option A is ruled out because the square-and-circle figure and the white drop are on opposite sides. Option C is ruled out because if it is folded so that the white drop is on top of the cube and the square-and-circle figure is at the front, then the black L-shape would be on the left. Option D is ruled out because the square-and-circle figure and the black L-shape are on opposite sides.

7. C
Option A is ruled out because the arrow should point towards the grey and white square. Option B is ruled out because if it is folded so that the grey and white square is on top of the cube and the white square is at the front, then the arrow would be on the left. Option D is ruled out because the grey and white square and the black arrow are on opposite sides.

8. D
Option A is ruled out because the white half of the black and white square should face the black and white circle. Option B is ruled out because if it is folded so that the grey oval is on top of the cube and the black and white square is at the front, then the black and white circle would be on the left. Option C is ruled out because the end of the oval should be facing the black and white circle.

9. B
The third cube view is the first cube view rotated 90 degrees left-to-right. So the face with the black triangle is on the top.

10. C
The third cube view is the second cube view rotated 90 degrees towards you, top-to-bottom, and then rotated 90 degrees anticlockwise in the plane of the page. So the white arrow is on the right.

11. A
The third cube view is the first cube view rotated 180 degrees in the plane of the page and then rotated 90 degrees left-to-right. So the black and grey circles are at the front.

12. D
The second cube view is the first cube view rotated 90 degrees away from you top-to-bottom, then rotated 90 degrees left-to-right. So the grey bars are on the left side of the cube. The third cube view is the second cube view rotated 90 degrees left-to-right, so the grey bars are at the front.

13.   **C**

The third cube view is the first cube view rotated 90 degrees right-to-left, then rotated 180 degrees in the plane of the page. So the white rectangle with the black square is on the right.

14.   **C**

Option C fits on the front of the figure.

15.   **A**

Option A fits on the right side of the figure.

16.   **D**

Option D rotates 90 degrees anticlockwise in the plane of the page. It then fits on the left of the figure.

17.   **B**

Option B rotates 90 degrees away from you, top-to-bottom, and then 90 degrees right-to-left. It then fits on the front of the figure.

Test 3 — pages 16-19

1.   **A**

The two bottom blocks in A are on the back left and front of the figure. The block at the top in A is at the back right of the figure.

2.   **C**

The top two blocks in C are at the front and back of the figure. The bottom block in C is the block in the middle of the figure.

3.   **A**

The top left block in A is at the front of the figure. The bottom right block in A is in the middle of the figure. The bottom left block in A is the block at the back of the figure.

4.   **D**

The top block in D is at the front of the figure. The bottom left block in D is in the middle of the figure. The bottom right block in D is at the back of the figure.

5.   **A**

Shape A has been rotated 90 degrees anticlockwise in the plane of the page.

6.   **B**

Shape B has been rotated 180 degrees towards you, top-to-bottom.

7.   **D**

Shape D has been rotated 90 degrees right-to-left.

8.   **C**

Shape C has been rotated 90 degrees towards you, top-to-bottom. It has then been rotated 90 degrees clockwise in the plane of the page.

9.   **E**

Shape E has been rotated 90 degrees right-to-left. It has then been rotated 180 degrees in the plane of the page.

10.   **F**

Shape F has been rotated 90 degrees towards you, top-to-bottom. It has then been rotated 90 degrees left-to-right.

11.   **C**

There are six blocks visible from above, which rules out options B and D. There are three blocks visible at the back, which rules out option A.

12.   **D**

There are five blocks visible from above, which rules out option B. There are three blocks visible on the left-hand side, which rules out option C. There is only one blue block visible from above, which rules out option A.

13.   **A**

There are six blocks visible from above, which rules out option B. There are three blocks visible at the back, which rules out option D. There is only one blue block visible from above, which rules out option C.

14.   **C**

There are six blocks visible from above, which rules out option B. There are three blocks visible at the front, which rules out option D. There is only one block visible on the left-hand side, which rules out option A.

15.   **A**

Options B and D are ruled out because there are no white side faces on the net. Option C is ruled out because the top rectangular face should be white.

16.   **C**

Option A is ruled out because the top square face should be blue. Option B is ruled out because if the blue trapezium is at the front, then the rectangular side should be white. Option D is ruled out because if the white trapezium is at the front, then the rectangular side should be blue.

17.   **A**

Option B is ruled out because there are no white triangular faces next to each other on the net. Option C is ruled out because there is only one grey triangular face on the net. Option D is ruled out because the two blue triangular faces should be next to each other.

18.   **B**

Option A is ruled out as the bottom right side should be white. Option C is ruled out because the top rectangular face should be white. Option D is ruled out because there is only one blue face on the net.

Puzzles 1 — page 20

Lost in Rotation

B. The view on Sally's left is the top-right figure rotated 90 degrees left-to-right. The view on her right is the top-left figure rotated 90 degrees right-to-left.

Pyramid Panic

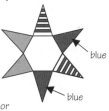

blue

blue

or

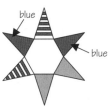

blue

blue

Test 4 — pages 21-24

1.   **B**

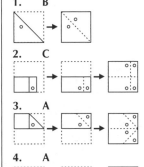

2.   **C**

3.   **A**

4.   **A**

5.   **B**

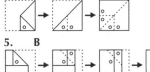

6.   **C**

The bottom block in C is the block at the bottom of the figure. The other block in C is on top of it.

7.   **D**

The bottom block in D goes at the back of the figure. The top left block in D is the block at the bottom right of the figure. The top right block in D is at the front of the figure.

8.   **A**

The top block in A is the block on the right of the figure. The bottom block in A goes at the bottom left of the figure. The other block in A goes on top of it.

9.   D
The top block in D is the block at the back of the figure. The other two blocks are arranged in front of it.

10.   B
There should be a blue cube at the top right of the figure, which rules out options A and C. The block on the left of the figure should be two cubes tall, which rules out option D.

11.   C
The block on the right when viewed from the left should be two cubes long and lying on its side. This rules out options A and B. There should be a block two cubes tall in the middle of the figure, which rules out option D.

12.   B
There should be just one cube at the top right when viewed from the left. This rules out options A and D. The block on the left should be three cubes tall, which rules out option C.

13.   D
There should be a block two cubes tall in the middle of the figure at the back when viewed from the left. This rules out options A and B. There should be a block two cubes tall on the right, which rules out option C.

14.   C
Option A is ruled out because the grey circle and black and white squares must be on opposite sides. Option B is ruled out because the grey face and white diamond must be on opposite sides. Option D is ruled out because there is no black circle on the net.

15.   B
Option A is ruled out because if the grey semicircle is on the top and the black semicircle is on the front, then the black stripe should be on the right. Option C is ruled out because there is no white pentagon on the net. Option D is ruled out because the hexagon and the black semicircle must be on opposite sides.

16.   A
Option B is ruled out because the black triangles should be pointing towards the oval. Option C is ruled out because the grey heart and the grey cross must be on opposite sides. Option D is ruled out because if the grey cross is on the top and the three black triangles are on the front, then the two black triangles should be on the right.

17.   A
Option B is ruled out because the grey arrow should be pointing towards the black diagonal line. Option C is ruled out because the black triangle and the black arrow must be on opposite sides. Option D is ruled out because the white triangle should be pointing towards the black triangle.

Test 5 — pages 25-28

1.   A
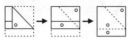

2.   C
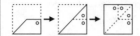

3.   A
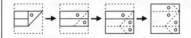

4.   C
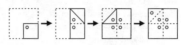

5.   C
The third cube view is the first cube view rotated 90 degrees clockwise in the plane of the page, and then 90 degrees away from you, top-to-bottom. So the white arch is on the front.

6.   D
The third cube view is the second cube view rotated 90 degrees left-to right. So the square is on the top.

7.   B
The second cube view is the first cube view rotated 90 degrees towards you, top-to-bottom. This means that the triangle on the third cube view must be on the opposite face to the grey and black stripe. So the third cube view is the first cube view rotated 90 degrees left-to-right. So the black part-circle is on the right.

8.   D
The third cube view is the second cube view rotated 90 degrees towards you, top-to-bottom, then 90 degrees clockwise in the plane of the page. This means that the double-headed arrow must be on the left of the third cube view and the cross must be on the bottom. The double-headed arrow points to both the cross and the heart, so the heart must be at the top.

9.   D
Shape D has been rotated 90 degrees clockwise in the plane of the page. It has then been rotated 90 degrees right-to-left.

10.   A
Shape A has been rotated 90 degrees towards you, top-to-bottom.

11.   F
Shape F has been rotated 180 degrees in the plane of the page.

12.   C
Shape C has been rotated 90 degrees right-to-left. It has then been rotated 180 degrees in the plane of the page.

13.   E
Shape E has been rotated 90 degrees away from you, top-to-bottom. It has then been rotated 90 degrees right-to-left.

14.   B
Shape B has been rotated 90 degrees away from you, top-to-bottom.

15.   A
The top two blocks in A are at the bottom of the figure. The cube is on the top.

16.   D
The top block in D is at the bottom of the figure. The bottom block in D is at the back of the figure on the left.

17.   B
The two left-hand blocks in B are arranged at the bottom of the figure. The right-hand block in B is at the top of the figure.

18.   D
The top block in D is standing at the front of the figure in the middle. The bottom left block in D is at the bottom left of the figure. The bottom right block in D is at the back of the figure.

Test 6 — pages 29-32

1.   C
There are six blocks visible from above, which rules out options A and D. There are only two blocks visible at the front, which rules out option B.

2.   D
There are five blocks visible from above, which rules out option A. There are three blocks visible on the right-hand side, which rules out option B. There are no blue blocks visible from above, which rules out option C.

3.   A
There are six blocks visible from above, which rules out option D. There is only one block visible on the right-hand side, which rules out option B. There is only one blue block visible from above, which rules out option C.

4.   B
There are six blocks visible from above, which rules out option D. There are two blocks visible on the middle row, which rules out option C. The two blocks on the middle row are not next to each other, which rules out option A.

5.   B
Option B fits at the back of the figure.

6.   B
Option B fits at the back right of the figure.

7.   C
Option C rotates 90 degrees anticlockwise in the plane of the page. It then fits on top of the figure.

8.   A
Option A rotates 90 degrees left-to-right. It then fits on top of the figure.

9.   C
Option A is ruled out because the net doesn't have a black circle. Option B is ruled out because the star and the grey and white circle must be on opposite sides. Option D is ruled out because the grey circle in a square and the grey hexagon must be on opposite sides.

10.   C
Option A is ruled out because the net does not have two grey arrows. Option B is ruled out because the black rectangles and the black triangles must be on opposite sides. Option D is ruled out because if the white star is on the front and the black rectangles are on top, then the white face must be on the left.

11.   B
Option A is ruled out because if the stars are on the top and the circle is on the front, then the black rectangles must be on the left. Option C is ruled out because the black rectangles and the grey and white rectangles must be on opposite sides. Option D is ruled out because the stars are in the wrong corners.

12.   C
Option A is ruled out because the diamond has been rotated. Option B is ruled out because the black cross and the two grey squares must be on opposite sides. Option D is ruled out because the grey trapezium and the black face must be on opposite sides.

13.   C
Option A is ruled out because the part of the figure originally to the right of the fold line is too small. Option B is ruled out because the part of the figure originally to the right of the fold line should still be visible. Option D is ruled out because the part of the figure that has been folded is the wrong shape.

14.   A
Option B is ruled out because the part of the figure that has not been folded is the wrong shape. Option C is ruled out because the part of the figure that has not been folded should still be visible. Option D is ruled out because the part of the figure that has been folded is the wrong shape.

15.   D
Option A is ruled out because the fold line has moved. Option B is ruled out because the part of the figure that has been folded is the wrong shape. Option C is ruled out because the part of the figure originally below the fold line should still be visible.

16.   D
Option A is ruled out because the part of the figure originally above the fold line has been rotated, not folded. Option B is ruled out because the part of the figure that has been folded is the wrong shape. Option C is ruled out because the part of the figure originally above the fold line should still be visible.

17.   C
Option A is ruled out because the part of the figure originally below the fold line is the wrong shape. Option B is ruled out because the fold line is in the wrong direction. Option D is ruled out because the part of the figure originally above the fold line should still be visible.

Puzzles 2 — page 33

Cube Conundrum
Net 1 will form the final cube for puzzle A. Puzzle B is puzzle A rotated 90 degrees clockwise in the plane of the page and then 90 degrees left-to-right. So the sun is on the bottom of Puzzle B.
This means that net 4 will form the final cube for puzzle B.

Folded Fox
C

Test 7 — pages 34-37

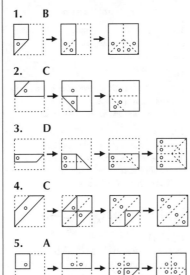

1.   B

2.   C

3.   D

4.   C

5.   A

6.   C
Options A and D are ruled out because the circular faces should be white. Option B is ruled out because the curved side of the cylinder should be blue.

7.   B
Option A is ruled out because the white rectangular face should be to the left of the grey triangular face. Option C is ruled out because the blue rectangular face should be to the left of the white triangular face. Option D is ruled out because there is no grey rectangular side on the net.

8.   A
Option B is ruled out because there is no grey rectangular face between two white rectangular faces on the net. Option C is ruled out because there is no grey rectangular face between two blue rectangular faces on the net. Option D is ruled out because there are not two grey rectangular faces next to each other on the net.

9.   C
Options A and B are ruled out because the top right-hand vertical square face should be white. Option D is ruled out because the horizontal square face on the left should be blue.

10.   C
There are five blocks visible from the right, which rules out option B. There are three blue blocks visible from the right, which rules out options A and D.

11.   B
There are five blocks visible from the right, which rules out option D. There is only one blue block visible from the right, which rules out option C. There is only one block visible on the right, which rules out option A.

12.   C
There are five blocks visible from the right, which rules out options B and D. There is only one block visible on the left, which rules out option A.

13.   C
There are seven blocks visible from the right, which rules out option D. There are three blocks visible on the left, which rules out option A. There are four blue blocks visible from the right, which rules out option B.

14.   D
Shape D has been rotated 90 degrees towards you, top-to-bottom.

15.   F
Shape F has been rotated 90 degrees right-to-left. It has then been rotated 90 degrees clockwise in the plane of the page.

16. E

Shape E has been rotated 180 degrees right-to-left.

17. B

Shape B has been rotated 90 degrees clockwise in the plane of the page. It has then been rotated 90 degrees right-to-left.

Test 8 — pages 38-41

1. C

There should be one block two cubes long on the right-hand side, going away from you, which rules out options A and B. The blue block should be in the centre at the back, which rules out option D.

2. D

There should be a block three cubes high on the back left, which rules out options A and B. One blue block should be visible from the back, which rules out option C.

3. B

There should be a block three cubes tall at the back right, which rules out options C and D. There should be a block two cubes tall at the front, which rules out option A.

4. C

There should be a cube at the front left, which rules out options B and D. There should be a block two cubes tall at the back left, which rules out option A.

5. C

Option A is ruled out because the part of the figure originally to the left of the fold line has been rotated. Option B is ruled out because the fold line has moved. Option D is ruled out because the part of the figure originally to the left of the fold line is the wrong shape.

6. A

Options B and D are ruled out because the part of the figure that has been folded is the wrong shape. Option C is ruled out because the part of the figure originally above the fold line should still be visible.

7. C

Option A is ruled out because the part of the figure originally above the fold line has been rotated. Option B is ruled out because the fold line is at the wrong angle. Option D is ruled out because the part of the figure originally above the fold line should still be visible.

8. C

Option A is ruled out because the fold line is in the wrong place. Option B is ruled out because the part of the figure originally below the fold line should still be visible. Option D is ruled out because the part of the figure originally above the fold line has been rotated, not folded.

9. B

Option A is ruled out because the part of the figure originally above the fold line has been rotated. Option C is ruled out because the part of the figure originally below the fold line should still be visible. Option D is ruled out because the part of the figure originally above the fold line is the wrong shape.

10. D

Options A and C are ruled out because the star and the cross are on opposite sides on the net. Option B is ruled out because the star and the square are on opposite sides on the net.

11. B

Option A is ruled out because the cross has been rotated. Option C is ruled out because the arrow has been rotated. Option D is ruled out because the wavy line and the arrow are on opposite sides on the net.

12. B

Option A is ruled out because the pentagon and the white star are on opposite sides on the net. Option C is ruled out because if it was folded so that the triangles are on the front of the cube and the white star is on top, then the pentagon would be on the bottom. Option D is ruled out because the pentagon has been rotated.

13. B

Option A is ruled out because if it was folded so that the squares are on the front of the cube and the circle is on top, then the hexagon must be on the left. Option C is ruled out because the circle has been rotated. Option D is ruled out because the squares have the wrong rotation.

14. B

Option B fits on top of the figure.

15. A

Option A fits on top and at the back of the figure.

16. D

Option D rotates 90 degrees clockwise in the plane of the page. It then fits at the bottom and on the left of the figure.

17. C

Option C rotates 90 degrees clockwise in the plane of the page, then 90 degrees away from you, top-to-bottom. It then fits at the back of the figure.

Test 9 — pages 42-45

1. D

There are four blocks visible from the back, which rules out option A. There are two blue blocks visible on the left-hand side when viewed from the back, which rules out options B and C.

2. C

There are six blocks visible from the back, which rules out option B. There is a blue block visible on the left-hand side when viewed from the back, which rules out options A and D.

3. D

There are five blocks visible from the back, which rules out option B. There are two blocks visible on the left when viewed from the back, which rules out option C. There is one block visible on top when viewed from the back, which rules out option A.

4. B

There are five blocks visible from the back, which rules out option A. There are two blocks visible at the top, which rules out option C. There are two blocks visible at the bottom, which rules out option D.

5. C

Option A is ruled out because there is no double-ended arrow on the net. Option B is ruled out because the net doesn't have two identical faces. Option D is ruled out because the two black squares and the black and white square must be on opposite sides.

6. B

Option A is ruled out because if the black cross is on the front and the white cross is on top, then the four-ended arrow must be on the left. Option C is ruled out because the black cross and the grey cross must be on opposite sides. Option D is ruled out because there's no grey square on the net.

7. B

Option A is ruled out because the small grey circle should be closest to the grey diamond. Option C is ruled out because if the grey and black stripes are on the front and the grey diamond is on top, then the black teardrop should be on the left. Option D is ruled out because the two teardrop shapes must be on opposite sides.

8. D

Option A is ruled out because the smaller end of the trapezium should be closest to the hexagons. Option B is ruled out because the face with the circles has been rotated. Option C is ruled out because the two circles and the pentagon must be on opposite sides.

9. F

Shape F has been rotated 90 degrees towards you, top-to-bottom.

10. A

Shape A has been rotated 180 degrees in the plane of the page.

11. D

Shape D has been rotated 90 degrees away from you, top-to-bottom.

12. E

Shape E has been rotated 90 degrees clockwise in the plane of the page. It has then been rotated 90 degrees right-to-left.

13. B

Shape B has been rotated 90 degrees away from you, top-to-bottom. It has then been rotated 90 degrees right-to-left.

14. C

Shape C has been rotated 90 degrees away from you, top-to-bottom. It has then been rotated 90 anticlockwise in the plane of the page.

15. A

The bottom block in A is the bottom block of the figure. The other two blocks are arranged above it.

16. C

The bottom block in C is the bottom left block of the figure. The middle block in C is the top right block in the figure. The top block in C is the block at the front of the figure.

17. D

The top block in D is the block at the back in the figure. The other two blocks are arranged in front of it.

18. D

The bottom block in D is at the front of the figure. The other two blocks are arranged behind it.

Puzzles 3 — page 46

Secret City
C

Robot Riddle
2

Test 10 — pages 47-50

1. A

The third cube view is the first cube view rotated 90 degrees right-to-left. So the face with the grey drop is at the front.

2. C

The third cube view is the first cube view rotated 90 degrees away from you, top-to-bottom. So the face with the white arrow is on the top.

3. B

The first cube view is the second cube view rotated 90 degrees towards you, top-to-bottom, and then rotated 90 degrees left-to-right. So the grey oval is at the bottom of the cube pointing towards the front and back faces. The third cube view is the first cube view rotated 180 degrees in the plane of the page, so the grey oval is on the top.

4. A

The second cube view is the first cube view rotated 90 degrees left-to-right, and then rotated 90 degrees anticlockwise in the plane of the page. So the grey cross is on the left. The third cube view is the second cube view rotated 90 degrees clockwise in the plane of the page, so the white arrow is on the right.

5. E

Shape E has been rotated 90 degrees clockwise in the plane of the page.

6. F

Shape F has been rotated 180 degrees right-to-left.

7. B

Shape B has been rotated 90 degrees anticlockwise in the plane of the page. It has then been rotated 90 degrees away from you, top-to-bottom.

8. C

Shape C has been rotated 180 degrees in the plane of the page. It has then been rotated 90 degrees right-to-left.

9. D

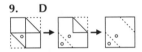

10. A

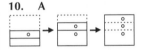

11. C

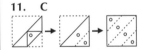

12. C

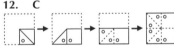

13. A

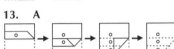

14. B

There are four blocks visible from the right, which rules out options A and D. There is only one block visible at the top, which rules out option C.

15. D

There are five blocks visible from the right, which rules out options B and C. There is only one blue block visible, which rules out option A.

16. B

There are five blocks visible from the right, which rules out option A. There are two blocks visible on the left, which rules out option C. There is only one block visible at the top, which rules out option D.

17. C

There are seven blocks visible from the right, which rules out option D. There are two blue blocks visible, which rules out option A. There are three blocks visible along the bottom, which rules out option B.

Test 11 — pages 51-54

1. C

Options A and B are ruled out because the fold lines have moved. Option D is ruled out because the part that has been folded is the wrong shape.

2. D

Option A is ruled out because the fold line has moved. Options B and C are ruled out because the parts that have been folded are the wrong shape.

3. B

Options A and C are ruled out because the parts that have been folded are the wrong shape. Option D is ruled out because the part that has been folded is too small.

4. D

Options A and C are ruled out because the parts that have been folded are the wrong shape. Option B is ruled out because the fold line has moved.

5. C

Options A and B are ruled out because the parts that have been folded are the wrong shape. Option D is ruled out because the part of the figure originally above the fold line has changed shape.

6. C

There should be a block three cubes high at the front right of the figure. This rules out options B and D. The only blue block should be a cube. This rules out option A.

7. D

There should be a cube at the top of the figure at the back. This rules out options A, B and C.

8. D

There should be a blue block two cubes long going into the page on the right of the figure. This should have a grey cube on top of it at the back. This rules out options A, B and C.

9. C

There should be a horizontal block two cubes long at the front left of the figure. This rules out options A, B and D.

10. A

Option B is ruled out because the triangular face on the right should be white. Option C is ruled out because the triangular face on the right should be grey. Option D is ruled out because there is no wide white triangular face.

11. C

Option A is ruled out because the face on the right should be white. Option B is ruled out because the face on the right should be blue. Option D is ruled out because the face on the right should be white.

12. A

Option B is ruled out because the upper sloped face should be grey and the lower sloped face should be white. Option C is ruled out because the top rectangular face should be grey. Option D is ruled out because the top rectangular face should be white.

13. C

Option A is ruled out because the two white rectangular faces should be next to each other. Option B is ruled out because the face to the right of the two white rectangular faces should be grey. Option D is ruled out because there should always be two white rectangular faces next to each other.

14. D

Option D fits on the front right of the figure.

15. C

Option C rotates 90 degrees anticlockwise in the plane of the page. It then fits at the front of the figure.

16. A

Option A rotates 90 degrees left-to-right. It then fits at the back of the figure.

17. B

Option B rotates 90 degrees anticlockwise in the plane of the page. It then rotates 90 degrees away from you, top-to-bottom. It then fits on the bottom of the figure.

Test 12 — pages 55-58

1. C

Shape C is rotated 90 degrees left-to-right. It is then rotated 90 degrees anticlockwise in the plane of the page.

2. F

Shape F is rotated 90 degrees left-to-right.

3. D

Shape D is rotated 90 degrees clockwise in the plane of the page. It is then rotated 90 degrees towards you, top-to-bottom.

4. A

Shape A is rotated 90 degrees towards you, top-to-bottom. It is then rotated 180 degrees right-to-left.

5. D

Option A is ruled out because the part of the figure originally left of the fold line has moved. Option B is ruled out because the part of the figure originally to the right of the fold line is the wrong shape. Option C is ruled out because the fold line has moved.

6. A

Option B is ruled out because the part of the figure originally below the fold line should be visible. Option C is ruled out because the part of the figure originally above the fold line should still be visible. Option D is ruled out because the fold line has moved.

7. B

Option A is ruled out because the part of the figure originally above the fold line has been rotated, not folded. Option C is ruled out because the part of the figure originally below the fold line is the wrong shape. Option D is ruled out because the fold line has moved.

8. B

Option A is ruled out because the part of the figure originally to the right of the fold line should still be visible. Option C is ruled out because the part of the figure originally to the left of the fold line is the wrong shape. Option D is ruled out because the part of the shape originally to the left of the fold line should still be visible.

9. D

Option A is ruled out because the part of the figure originally to the left of the fold line should still be visible. Option B is ruled out because the part of the figure that has been folded is the wrong shape. Option C is ruled out because the part of the figure that has not been folded is the wrong shape.

10. C

Option C fits at the back of the figure.

11. D

Option D fits at the bottom of the figure.

12. C

Option C rotates 90 degrees anticlockwise in the plane of the page. It then fits at the back of the figure.

13. B

Option B rotates 90 degrees right-to-left, then 180 degrees in the plane of the page. It then fits at the front of the figure.

14. D

Option A is ruled out because the black diamond and the grey circle must be on opposite sides. Option B is ruled out because the grey face and the white face must be on opposite sides. Option C is ruled out because there is no black pentagon on the net.

15. A

Option B is ruled out because the cross and the star must be on opposite sides. Option C is ruled out because if the black rectangles are at the front and the black cross is on top, then the circles must be on the left. Option D is ruled out because the rectangles have been rotated.

16. B

Option A is ruled out because if the E-shape is at the front and the O-shape is on top, then the Z-shape must be on the left. Option C is ruled out because the L-shape has been rotated. Option D is ruled out because the T-shape and the E-shape must be on opposite sides.

17. A

Option B is ruled out because the two triangles have been rotated. Option C is ruled out because the semicircle and the grey triangle must be on opposite sides. Option D is ruled out because if the black rectangles are on the front and the circle is on top, then the semicircle must be on the left.

Puzzles 4 — page 59

Folding and Holding (Hands)
1. B
2. C
3. D

Test 13 — pages 60-63

1. A

Option B is ruled out because the figure has been broken apart along the fold line. Option C is ruled out because the fold line has moved. Option D is ruled out because the part of the figure that has been folded is the wrong shape.

2. B

Option A is ruled out because the part of the figure originally below the fold line should not still be visible. Option C is ruled out because the fold line has moved. Option D is ruled out because the part of the figure originally below the fold line is the wrong shape.

3. C

Option A is ruled out because the part of the figure that has not been folded is the wrong shape. Option B is ruled out because the part of the figure that has been folded is the wrong shape. Option D is ruled out because the part of the figure originally to the left of the fold line should still be visible.

4. B

Option A is ruled out because the part of the figure that has not been folded is the wrong shape. Options C and D are ruled out because the fold line has moved.

5. D

Options A and C are ruled out because the fold line has moved. Option B is ruled out because the part of the figure originally to the right of the fold line has been rotated, not folded.

6. C

Option A is ruled out because the squares and the arrow are on opposite sides. Option B is ruled out because the arrow and the triangle are on opposite sides. Option D is ruled out because there is no hexagon on the cube.

7. C

Option A is ruled out because the cross and the square are on opposite sides. Option B is ruled out because if it is folded so that the circles are on the front of the cube and the square is on top, the cross would be on the left. Option D is ruled out because the circles and the square are on opposite sides.

8. A

Option B is ruled out because if it is folded so that the diamond is on the front of the cube and the grey face is on top, the ovals would be on the left. Option C is ruled out because the diamond and the ovals are on opposite sides. Option D is ruled out because the narrow ends of the ovals should point towards the grey face.

9. C

Option A is ruled out because if it is folded so that the grey arrow is at the front of the cube and the white arrow is on top, the black arrow would be pointing down. Option B is ruled out because the black arrow should be pointing the opposite way to the grey arrow. Option D is ruled out because if it is folded so that the grey arrow is on the front of the cube and the black arrow is on the right, then the white arrow would be pointing to the left.

10. C

The third cube view is the first cube view rotated 90 degrees anticlockwise in the plane of the page, then 90 degrees left-to-right. So the face with the black arrow is on top.

11. B

The third cube view is the second cube view rotated 90 degrees clockwise in the plane of the page, then 90 degrees away from you, top-to-bottom. So the face with the cross is at the front.

12. A

The second cube view is the first cube view rotated 180 degrees in the plane of the page, then 90 degrees away from you, top-to-bottom, so the pentagon is on the left. This means that the third cube view is the second cube view rotated 90 degrees anticlockwise in the plane of the page, so the two squares are on top.

13. B

The second cube view is the first cube view rotated 180 degrees in the plane of the page, so the T-shape is opposite the arrow and the grey rectangle is opposite the L-shape. The third cube view is the first cube view rotated 90 degrees anticlockwise in the plane of the page. So the T-shape must be on the left of the cube, meaning the white arrow is on the right.

14. C

There should be a block three cubes high at the back left of the figure, which rules out options A and B. There should be a blue block at the back right of the figure, which rules out option D.

15. D

There should be a block three cubes high on the right of the figure, which rules out options A and C. There should be a block two cubes high behind it, which rules out option B.

16. C

There should be a block three cubes long at the front of the figure, which rules out options A and B. There should be one cube at the back right of the figure, which rules out option D.

17. D

There should be a block two cubes high on the left of the figure, which rules out options A and C. There should be just one block at the front of the figure, in front of the others, which rules out option B.

Test 14 — pages 64-67

1. A

The top right block in A goes at the bottom left of the figure. The bottom right block in A goes at the bottom right of the figure. The other block goes on the top of the figure.

2. B

The bottom block in B goes at the bottom right of the figure. The middle block in B goes on top of it. The top block in B goes at the back of the figure.

3. D

The top block in D goes at the back of the figure. The bottom left block in D goes at the front of the figure and the other block goes on top of it.

4. A

The top block in A goes at the back of the figure. The other two blocks are arranged in front of and underneath it.

5. C

Shape C has been rotated 90 degrees left-to-right.

6. D

Shape D has been rotated 90 degrees towards you, top-to-bottom.

7. E

Shape E has been rotated 180 degrees right-to-left.

8. B

Shape B has been rotated 90 degrees anticlockwise in the plane of the page. It has then been rotated 90 degrees towards you, top-to-bottom.

9. F

Shape F has been rotated 90 degrees left-to-right. It has then been rotated 90 degrees clockwise in the plane of the page.

10. A

Shape A has been rotated 180 degrees towards you, top-to-bottom. It has then been rotated 90 degrees right-to-left.

11. B

There are five blocks visible from the left, which rules out options C and D. There are two blocks visible on the left, which rules out option A.

12. A

There are six blocks visible from the left, which rules out options B and C. There are three blocks visible along the bottom, which rules out option D.

13. D

There are five blocks visible from the left, which rules out option A. There is only one block visible on the left, which rules out options B and C.

14. A

There are six blocks visible from the left, which rules out option C. There is no blue block in the middle of the figure, which rules out option B. There are two blocks visible on the left, which rules out option D.

15. C

Option A is ruled out because there is no black circle. Option B is ruled out because the arrow and the rectangle must be on opposite sides. Option D is ruled out because the grey face and the black square must be on opposite sides.

16. B

Option A is ruled out because if the grey triangle is on the front and the black three-pointed star is on the top, then the black cross should be on the right. Option C is ruled out because the grey triangle and the white square must be on opposite sides. Option D is ruled out because there is no white diamond.

17. D

Option A is ruled out because the black circle and the black arrow must be on opposite sides. Option B is ruled out because the top edge of the T-shape should be next to the triangle. Option C is ruled out because if the white triangle is on the front and the grey trapezium is on the top, then the black arrow should be on the right.

18.   C

Option A is ruled out because the arrow should point towards the bottom. Option B is ruled out because if the two black stripes are on the front and the semicircle is on the top, then the drop should be on the right. Option D is ruled out because the arrow should point away from the star.

Test 15 — pages 68-71

1.   C

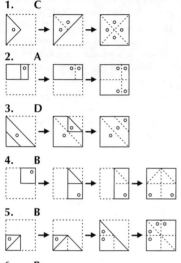

2.   A

3.   D

4.   B

5.   B

6.   B

The cube should be at the front of the figure when viewed from the back, which rules out option A. The block on the right should be two cubes tall, which rules out option C. The block on the right should be at the back, which rules out option D.

7.   C

The cube should be at the back of the figure when viewed from the back, which rules out option B. The block on the bottom left should not be in front of the other blocks, which rules out option A. The upright block should be on the right of the figure, which rules out option D.

8.   D

The block on the right should not be at the front of the figure when viewed from the back, which rules out option A. The upright block at the front should be lower than the upright block at the back, which rules out option B. The block at the front should be in the middle, which rules out option C.

9.   B

The block on the left is two cubes long, which rules out option A. The upright block in the middle of the figure should be at the back, which rules out option C. The block on the left should be at the front, which rules out option D.

10.   A

The bottom block in A is the block on the front left of the figure. The middle block in A goes to the right of it and the top block in A goes behind it.

11.   B

The top block in B is the block on the right of the figure. The other two blocks in B are arranged to the left of it.

12.   D

The bottom block in D is the block at the front of the figure, on the bottom. The other two blocks in D are arranged behind and on top of it.

13.   C

The top right block in C has been rotated 90 degrees clockwise in the plane of the page to become the block at the back of the figure. The bottom two blocks in C are arranged in front of it. The cube can either go on the right or at the bottom of the figure, depending on how the bottom two blocks in C are arranged.

14.   A

Option B is ruled out because the rectangular face on top of the shape should be white. Option C is ruled out because there is no grey trapezium face on the net. Option D is ruled out because there is no blue short rectangular face on the net.

15.   B

Option A is ruled out because the square face on top of the shape should be white. Option C is ruled out because there are no white rectangular faces next to each other on the net. Option D is ruled out because there are no grey faces next to each other on the net.

16.   C

Option A is ruled out because the grey rectangular face should be blue. Options B and D are ruled out because the grey face on the right of the shape should be white.

17.   D

Option A is ruled out because the grey square face on the right of the shape should be white. Option B is ruled out because the top vertical square face should be blue. Option C is ruled out because the square face on top of the shape should not be blue.

Puzzles 5 — page 72

Creepy Crawlies
D
Castle Catastrophe
15

Test 16 — pages 73-76

1.   B

There are four blocks visible from the back, which rules out options A and C. There are three blocks visible on the bottom, which rules out option D.

2.   C

There are six blocks visible from the back, which rules out option D. There are two blue blocks visible from the back, which rules out option B. There is one block visible on the left when viewed from the back, which rules out option A.

3.   B

There are five blocks visible from the back, which rules out option C. There is one blue block visible from the back, which rules out options A and D.

4.   C

There are six blocks visible from the back, which rules out option A. There are two blocks visible on the right when viewed from the back, which rules out option D. There are three blocks visible on the middle row, which rules out option B.

5.   D

Option A is ruled out because the circle and the arrow are on opposite sides on the net. Option B is ruled out because the cross and the rectangle are on opposite sides on the net. Option C is ruled out because there is no white cross on the net.

6.   B

Option A is ruled out because the grey semicircles and the white circles are on opposite sides on the net. Option C is ruled out because the grey semicircles have been rotated. Option D is ruled out because the star and the black circle are on opposite sides on the net.

7.   A

Option B is ruled out because the white teardrop shape has been rotated. Option C is ruled out because the curved line and the white teardrop shape are on opposite sides on the net. Option D is ruled out because if the black rectangles are at the front and the curved line is on the right, then the grey teardrop would be on top.

8.   C

Option A is ruled out because the H-shape has been rotated. Option B is ruled out because if the H-shape is at the front and the black three pointed shape is on the right, the white shape should be underneath. Option D is ruled out because the white shape has been rotated.

9.   A

Shape A is rotated 90 degrees clockwise in the plane of the page.

10.   C

Shape C is rotated 90 degrees right-to-left.

11.   B

Shape B is rotated 90 degrees towards you, top-to-bottom. It is then rotated 90 degrees anticlockwise, in the plane of the page.

12.   F

Shape F is rotated 180 degrees towards you, top-to-bottom.

13.   D

Shape D is rotated 90 degrees towards you, top-to-bottom. It is then rotated 180 degrees right-to-left.

14.   E

Shape E is rotated 90 degrees right-to-left. It is then rotated 90 degrees clockwise in the plane of the page.

15.   D

Option D fits on the top right of the figure.

16.   C

Option C fits at the back of the figure.

17.   B

Option B is rotated 180 degrees left-to-right. It then fits on the right of the figure.

18.   A

Option A is rotated 90 degrees away from you, top-to-bottom, then 90 degrees left-to-right. It then fits at the back of the figure.

Test 17 — pages 77-80

1.   D

There should be a vertical block three cubes high at the front left of the figure, which rules out option B. There should be a horizontal block three cubes long on the bottom right of the figure, which rules out option C. The front of the figure should be flat, which rules out option A.

2.   A

There should be a blue block two cubes long at the front left of the figure, which rules out options B and C. There should be a cube visible at the back of the figure on the top right, which rules out option D.

3.   B

There should be a blue block two cubes long at the bottom left of the figure, which rules out option C. There should be nothing on top of the front half of this blue block, which rules out option A. There should be a horizontal grey block two cubes long on the top right of the figure, which rules out option D.

4.   C

There should be a blue block with nothing directly in front of it, which rules out option A. This blue block should extend all the way to the left edge of the figure, which rules out option B. The two grey blocks at the top of the figure should only be touching at their corners, which rules out option D.

5.   D

Options A and C are ruled out because the triangular face at the front should be blue. Option B is ruled out because the triangular face on the left should be white.

6.   C

Option A is ruled out because the blue face has been reflected. Options B and D are ruled out because the front face should be white and the right face should be grey.

7.   C

Options A and B are ruled out because the lower face on the left should be white. Option D is ruled out because the lower face on the right should be white.

8.   A

Option B is ruled out because the lowest visible horizontal face should be grey. Option C is ruled out because the white faces should be grey and the grey faces should be white. Option D is ruled out because there should not be two small grey square faces.

9.   B

The third cube view is the first cube view rotated 90 degrees away from you, top-to-bottom, then 90 degrees right-to-left. So the E-shape is on the right.

10.   C

The third cube view is the second cube view rotated 90 degrees right-to-left. So the black star is at the front.

11.   A

The second cube view is the first cube view rotated 180 degrees right-to-left, so the black triangle is on the left. The third cube view is the second cube view rotated 90 degrees clockwise in the plane of the page. So the black triangle is on the top.

12.   D

The first cube view is the second cube view rotated 90 degrees towards you, top-to-bottom, then 90 degrees left-to-right, so the wavy flag shape is on the bottom. The third cube view is the first cube view rotated 180 degrees in the plane of the page. So the wavy flag shape is on the top.

13.   A

Option B is ruled out because the fold line is in the wrong direction. Option C is ruled out because the fold line has moved. Option D is ruled out because the part that has been folded is the wrong shape.

14.   D

Option A is ruled out because the part of the figure originally to the right of the fold line should still be visible. Option B is ruled out because the part that has been folded is the wrong shape. Option C is ruled out because the fold line has moved.

15.   B

Option A is ruled out because the part that has been folded is the wrong shape. Option C is ruled out because the fold line has moved. Option D is ruled out because the part of the figure originally to the right of the fold line should still be visible.

16.   C

Option A is ruled out because the part of the figure originally above the fold line is the wrong shape. Option B is ruled out because the fold line has moved. Option D is ruled out because the parts that have been folded are the wrong shape.

17.   A

Option B is ruled out because the part that has been folded is the wrong shape. Option C is ruled out because the part of the figure originally to the right of the fold line should still be visible. Option D is ruled out because the fold line has moved.

Test 18 — pages 81-84

1.   B

Shape B has been rotated 90 degrees right-to-left.

2.   A

Shape A has been rotated 180 degrees right-to-left.

3.   F

Shape F has been rotated 90 degrees towards you, top-to-bottom. It has then been rotated 90 degrees right-to-left.

4.   D

Shape D has been rotated 90 degrees right-to-left. It has then been rotated 180 degrees in the plane of the page.

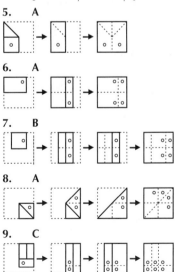

5.   A

6.   A

7.   B

8.   A

9.   C

10. B

The top block in B is on the top of the figure. The other two blocks are arranged underneath.

11. A

The top right block in A is the front block of the figure. The other two blocks are arranged behind it.

12. B

The bottom right block in B is at the back of the figure. The other two blocks are arranged in front of it.

13. D

The bottom block in D is the front block in the middle of the figure. The block on the right in D is on the right of the figure. The top block in D is at the back of the figure.

14. D

There are five blocks visible from the left, which rules out options A and C. There are two blocks visible at the top, which rules out option B.

15. A

There are four blocks visible from the left, which rules out option B. There is one blue block visible from the left, which rules out options C and D.

16. C

There are five blocks visible from the left, which rules out option B. There is only one block visible at the top, which rules out options A and D.

17. B

There are five blocks visible from the left, which rules out option D. There is only one block visible on the right, which rules out option C. There is only one block visible at the top, which rules out option A.

Puzzles 6 — page 85

Creased Shirts

Jerry's shirt — B

Terry's shirt — G

Kerry's shirt — I

Plane Sailing

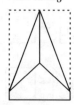

Test 19 — pages 86-89

1. C

Option A is ruled out because the folded shape has been stretched horizontally. Option B is ruled out because the fold line has moved. Option D is ruled out because the part of the figure originally to the right of the fold line should still be visible.

2. B

Option A is ruled out because the part of the figure that was below the fold line has been rotated, not folded. Option C is ruled out because the part of the figure originally below the fold line should still be visible. Option D is ruled out because the part of the figure originally above the fold line is too small.

3. D

Option A is ruled out because the part of the figure that has been folded is the wrong shape. Option B is ruled out because the fold line has moved. Option C is ruled out because the part of the figure originally to the right of the fold line should still be visible.

4. D

Option A is ruled out because the part of the figure originally above the fold line should still be visible. Option B is ruled out because the part of the figure that hasn't been folded is the wrong shape. Option C is ruled out because the fold line has moved.

5. A

Option B is ruled out because the part of the figure that has been folded is the wrong shape. Option C is ruled out because the fold line has moved. Option D is ruled out because the part of the figure originally above the fold line should still be visible.

6. B

Option A is ruled out because the white circle and the grey stripe must be on opposite sides. Option C is ruled out because the hearts and the hexagon must be on opposite sides. Option D is ruled out because there is no black circle.

7. D

Option A is ruled out because the grid squares and the heart must be on opposite sides. Option B is ruled out because the black arch shapes have been rotated. Option C is ruled out because if the white cross is on the top and the heart is on the front, then the black arch shapes should be on the right.

8. D

Option A is ruled out because the semicircle and the cross should be on opposite sides. Option B is ruled out because if the triangle is on the top and the diamond is on the front, then the cross should be on the right. Option C is ruled out because there is no kite shape.

---

9. C

Option A is ruled out because the two flat sides of the arch should face the arrow. Option B is ruled out because if the pentagon is at the front and the arrow is on the top, then the F shape should be on the right. Option D is ruled out because the fatter end of the curved white shape should be closest to the pentagon.

10. B

Option B fits behind the figure.

11. D

Option D is rotated 90 degrees right-to-left, then fits on top of the figure at the back.

12. A

Option A is rotated 180 degrees clockwise in the plane of the page. It then fits at the back of the figure.

13. B

Option B is rotated 90 degrees clockwise in the plane of the page, then 90 degrees left-to-right. It then fits on the right of the figure at the front.

14. D

On the left of the figure at the back, there should be a blue block three cubes long. This rules out option A. On the right of the figure at the back, there should be a grey block two cubes long. This rules out option B. There should be a block three cubes long across the front of the figure. This rules out option C.

15. B

On the top right of the figure there should be a blue cube. This rules out options A and C. This blue cube should be at the front of the figure. This rules out option D.

16. B

There should be a blue block two cubes long with a grey cube in front of it. This rules out options A and C. This blue block should also have a cube to the left of it. This rules out option D.

17. C

There should be a blue block two cubes long going into the page at the top left of the figure. This rules out options A and D. There should be a grey block three cubes long across the centre of the figure at the back. This rules out option B.

Test 20 — pages 90-93

1. C

The bottom block in C is at the front of the figure. The other two blocks are arranged behind it.

2. A

The bottom block in A is at the front of the figure. The middle block in A goes above it and the cube goes behind it.

---

3.   D
The bottom block in D is at the front right of the figure. The top block goes behind it and the middle block goes to the left of it.

4.   C
The bottom block in C is at the front of the figure. The other two blocks are arranged behind it.

5.   A
Option B is ruled out because the figure has been broken apart along the fold line. Option C is ruled out because the fold line has moved. Option D is ruled out because the part of the figure that has been folded is the wrong shape.

6.   A
Option B is ruled out because the fold line has moved. Option C is ruled out because the part of the figure that has not been folded is the wrong shape. Option D is ruled out because the part of the figure originally above the fold line should still be visible.

7.   B
Option A is ruled out because the part of the figure originally above the fold line should still be visible. Option C is ruled out because the part of the figure that has not been folded is the wrong shape. Option D is ruled out because the fold line has moved.

8.   D
Option A is ruled out because the part of the figure originally to the left of the fold line should still be visible. Option B is ruled out because the part of the figure that has been folded is the wrong shape. Option C is ruled out because the fold line has moved.

9.   C
Option A is ruled out because the part of the figure that has not been folded is the wrong shape. Option B is ruled out because the part of the figure originally below the fold line has been rotated, not folded. Option D is ruled out because the part of the figure that has been folded is the wrong shape.

10.   B
There are four blocks visible from the right, which rules out option C. There are two blocks visible on the right, which rules out option A. There are three blocks visible at the bottom, which rules out option D.

11.   D
There are no blue blocks visible from the right, which rules out options A and C. There is only one block visible at the top, which rules out option B.

12.   B
There are five blocks visible from the right, which rules out option A. There are three blocks visible at the top, which rules out option C. There are two blocks visible on the left, which rules out option D.

13.   D
There are seven blocks visible from the right, which rules out option C. There are only two blocks visible on the right, which rules out options A and B.

14.   B
The third cube is the second cube rotated 90 degrees clockwise in the plane of the page, then 90 degrees away from you, top-to-bottom. So the pentagon is on top.

15.   A
The third cube is the second cube rotated 90 degrees right-to-left and then 90 degrees clockwise in the plane of the page. So the circle is on the right.

16.   B
The second cube is the first cube rotated 180 degrees right-to-left. The third cube is the second cube rotated 90 degrees right-to-left. So the black squares are on the right.

17.   A
The second cube is the first cube rotated 90 degrees towards you, top-to-bottom, so the square is on the bottom. The third cube view is the second cube view rotated 180 degrees towards you, top-to-bottom, so the square is at the top.

Test 21 — pages 94-97

1.   C
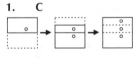

2.   D
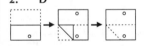

3.   C
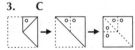

4.   A
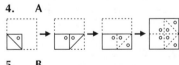

5.   B
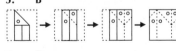

6.   B
Options A, C and D are ruled out because there are no grey triangular or wide rectangular faces.

7.   D
Option A is ruled out because the blue triangular face should be next to a grey triangular face. Option B is ruled out because the grey triangular faces should be on opposite sides of the pyramid. Option C is ruled out because there is only one white triangular face.

8.   D
Option A is ruled out because the top rectangular face should be white. Option B is ruled out because the sloping rectangular face should be grey. Option C is ruled out because the trapezium face should be grey.

9.   D
Option A is ruled out because the two blue square faces cannot be next to each other. Option B is ruled out because if the white pentagon is on top, the blue square face should be to the right of the grey square face. Option C is ruled out because the two white squares cannot be next to each other.

10.   A
Option A fits behind the figure.

11.   C
Option C fits on the back left of the figure.

12.   A
Option A is rotated 90 degrees right-to-left, then fits on top of the figure.

13.   B
Option B is rotated 180 degrees right-to-left, then fits on the right of the figure.

14.   C
There are three blocks visible from the top, which rules out options A and B. There are two rows when viewed from above, which rules out option D.

15.   A
There are five blocks visible from the top, which rules out options B and C. There are two blocks visible on the right, which rules out option D.

16.   D
There are six blocks visible from the top, which rules out option C. There are three blocks visible at the front, which rules out options A and B.

17.   B
There are five blocks visible from the top, which rules out option A. There are two blocks visible at the front, which rules out options C and D.

Puzzles 7 — page 98

Hairy Heights
Trevor

Perky Penguin

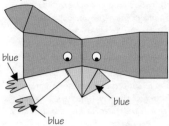

blue

blue

blue

Test 22 — pages 99-102

1.   D
Shape D has been rotated 90 degrees towards you, top-to-bottom.

2.   F
Shape F has been rotated 90 degrees clockwise in the plane of the page. It has then been rotated 90 degrees right-to-left.

3.   C
Shape C has been rotated 90 degrees left-to-right. It has then been rotated 90 degrees towards you, top-to-bottom.

4.   A
Shape A has been rotated 180 degrees in the plane of the page. It has then been rotated 90 degrees right-to-left.

5.   B
Shape B fits on the back of the figure.

6.   C
Shape C fits on the left of the figure.

7.   A
Shape A is rotated 90 degrees clockwise in the plane of the page. It then fits on top of the figure.

8.   C
Shape C is rotated 90 degrees clockwise in the plane of the page and then 90 degrees away from you, top-to-bottom. It then fits on the front of the figure.

9.   C
Option A is ruled out because there is no grey square on the cube. Option B is ruled out because the trapezium and the heart are on opposite sides. Option D is ruled out because the heart and the semicircle are on opposite sides.

10.   A
Option B is ruled out because the arrow shape and the black bar with the circle are on opposite sides. Option C is ruled out because the arrow shape should be pointing towards the black bar with the circle. Option D is ruled out because one end of the black bar should be pointing towards the grey cross shape.

11.   D
Option A is ruled out because the straight sides of the arch shape should be furthest from the black bars. Option B is ruled out because if it is folded so that the grey triangle is on the front of the cube and the arch is on the top, then the black bars would be on the left. Option C is ruled out because the triangle should be pointing away from the arch.

12.   B
Option A is ruled out because the grey half of the square should be closest to the arrowhead. Option C is ruled out because one end of the white bar on top of the grey ring should be pointing towards the grey and white square. Option D is ruled out because if it is folded so that the black arrow is on the front of the cube and the grey and white square is on the right, then the white bar with the grey ring would be on the bottom.

13.   D

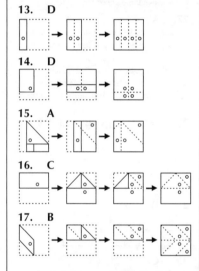

14.   D

15.   A

16.   C

17.   B

Test 23 — pages 103-106

1.   B
The bottom block in B is at the bottom of the figure. The other two blocks are arranged above and behind it.

2.   C
The bottom block in C is at the front of the figure. The other two blocks are arranged behind it.

3.   D
The top block in D is at the back left of the figure. The other two blocks are arranged to the right of it.

4.   D
The bottom block in D is at the bottom of the figure at the front. The top left block in D goes behind it and the top right block goes above it on the left.

5.   B
Option A is ruled out because the part of the figure that has not been folded is the wrong shape. Option C is ruled out because the part of the figure originally above the fold line still be visible. Option D is ruled out because the figure has been broken apart along the fold line.

6.   A
Option B is ruled out because the part of the figure that has not been folded is the wrong shape. Option C is ruled out because the fold line has moved. Option D is ruled out because the part of the figure originally to the left of the fold line has been rotated, not folded.

7.   C
Option A is ruled out because the part of the figure that has been folded is the wrong shape. Option B is ruled out because the part of the figure originally to the left of the fold line should still be visible. Option D is ruled out because the part of the figure that has not been folded is the wrong shape.

8.   C
Option A is ruled out because the fold line has moved. Option B is ruled out because the part of the figure that has been folded is the wrong shape. Option D is ruled out because the part of the figure originally above the fold line should still be visible.

9.   C
Option A is ruled out because the part of the figure that has not been folded is the wrong shape. Option B is ruled out because the fold line has moved. Option D is ruled out because the part of the figure that has been folded is the wrong shape.

10.   D
There should be a block three blocks tall on the right of the figure, which rules out options A and C. There should be a blue block two cubes long lying on its side, which rules out option B.

11.   B
There should be a block two cubes long lying on its side at the front of the figure, which rules out option C. There should not be any blue blocks on the left-hand side, which rules out options A and D.

12.   A
There should be a block two cubes tall on the left-hand side, which rules out options C and D. There should be a block two cubes long lying on its side at the back of the figure, which rules out option B.

13.   D
There should be a block three cubes long lying on its side in the middle of the figure, which rules out option B. There should be a single cube at the back of the figure at the bottom, which rules out option C. There should be a block two cubes long at the back right of the figure, which rules out option A.

14. B
The third cube is the second cube rotated 90 degrees towards you, top-to-bottom, then 90 degrees anticlockwise in the plane of the page. So the parallelogram is on the right.

15. D
The third cube is the first cube rotated 90 degrees clockwise in the plane of the page, then 90 degrees away from you, top-to-bottom. So the hexagon is at the front.

16. B
The third cube is the second cube rotated 90 degrees anticlockwise in the plane of the page, then 180 degrees right-to-left. So the quarter circle is on top.

17. C
The second cube is the first cube rotated 180 degrees towards you, top-to-bottom. So the Z-shape is at the bottom. The third cube is the second cube rotated 90 degrees clockwise in the plane of the page, then 90 degrees left-to-right. So the Z-shape is on the front.

Test 24 — pages 107-110

1. B
There are five blocks visible from the top, which rules out options A and D. There are two blocks visible at the front, which rules out option C.

2. D
There are five blocks visible from the top, which rules out options A and B. There is one blue block visible, which rules out option C.

3. B
There are five blocks visible from the top, which rules out option C. There is only one blue block visible, which rules out option A. There are two blocks visible on the left, which rules out option D.

4. C
There are six blocks visible from the top, which rules out option B. There is one blue block visible, which rules out option D. The blue block is visible on the middle row, which rules out option A.

5. A
Shape A fits on the left side of the figure.

6. C
Shape C fits on the right side of the figure.

7. C
Shape C is rotated 90 degrees clockwise in the plane of the page. It then fits on the front of the figure.

8. B
Shape B rotates 90 degrees anticlockwise in the plane of the page and then 90 degrees left-to-right. It then fits on the right side of the figure.

9. C
Shape C has been rotated 90 degrees away from you, top-to-bottom.

10. F
Shape F has been rotated 90 degrees right-to-left.

11. E
Shape E has been rotated 90 degrees clockwise in the plane of the page.

12. B
Shape B has been rotated 180 degrees, top-to-bottom.

13. A
Shape A has been rotated 90 degrees right-to-left. It has then been rotated 90 degrees away from you, top-to-bottom.

14. D
Shape D has been rotated 90 degrees anticlockwise in the plane of the page. It has then been rotated 90 degrees left-to-right.

15. B
Option A is ruled out because the square-and-circle figure and the five circles must be on opposite sides. Option C is ruled out because the net does not have a grey heart. Option D is ruled out because the grey face and the grey bars must be on opposite sides.

16. C
Option A is ruled out because the black face and the circles-and-lines figure must be on opposite sides. Option B is ruled out because if the circles-and-lines figure is on the front and the white bars are on the top, then the grey oval should be on the right. Option D is ruled out because the grey ring and the grey oval must be on opposite sides.

17. D
Option A is ruled out because the white square has been rotated. Option B is ruled out because the two black squares should be closest to the arrow. Option C is ruled out because if the grey arrow is on the front and the white square is on the top, then the squares-and-lines figure should be on the right.

18. B
Option A is ruled out because the black stripe has been rotated. Option C is ruled out because if the black rectangle is on the front and the triangle is on the right, then the four grey circles should be on the top. Option D is ruled out because the white cross shape has been rotated.

Puzzles 8 — page 111

Block Cat
D. Its back legs have swapped places.

Cube Chaos
1.

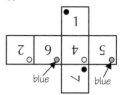

2.

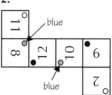

Test 25 — pages 112-115

1. A
The third cube view is the first cube view rotated 90 degrees anticlockwise in the plane of the page, then 90 degrees left-to-right. So the face with the circle is on top.

2. D
The third cube view is the first cube view rotated 90 degrees right-to-left, then 90 degrees clockwise in the plane of the page. So the black circle with the line across it is on top.

3. C
The third cube view is the first cube view rotated 90 degrees towards you, top-to-bottom. So the hexagons are on the right.

4. A
The second cube view is the first cube view rotated 90 degrees clockwise in the plane of the page, then 90 degrees right-to-left. So the two circles are on the left. This means that the third cube view is the second cube view rotated 180 degrees right-to-left, so the grey cross is on top.

5. B
Options A and D are ruled out because there are no large blue rectangular faces on the net. Option C is ruled out because the top small rectangular face should be white.

6. D
Option A is ruled out because the triangular face should be blue. Option B is ruled out because the triangular face should be grey. Option C is ruled out because the large rectangular face should be white.

7.   B

Option A is ruled out because there is only one grey rectangular face on the net. Option C is ruled out because the blue rectangular face should be white. Option D is ruled out because there are no blue rectangular faces next to each other on the net.

8.   D

Option A is ruled out because the top rectangular face should be blue. Option B is ruled out because the large rectangular face should be grey. Option C is ruled out because the trapezium-shaped face should be blue.

9.   B

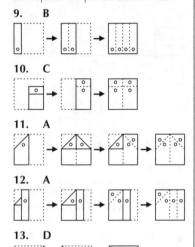

10.   C

11.   A

12.   A

13.   D

14.   C

Shape C fits on top of the figure at the front.

15.   D

Shape D fits on the right of the figure.

16.   B

Shape B is rotated 90 degrees right-to-left. It then fits underneath the figure.

17.   A

Shape A is rotated 90 degrees right-to-left. It then fits on the front right of the figure.

Test 26 — pages 116-119

1.   B

There are four blocks visible from the back, which rules out options C and D. There are two blocks visible on the right when viewed from the back, which rules out option A.

2.   B

There are six blocks visible from the back, which rules out options C and D. There are two blocks visible on the left when viewed from the back, which rules out option A.

3.   D

There are six blocks visible from the back, which rules out option A. There are two blocks visible at the bottom when viewed from the back, which rules out options B and C.

4.   A

There are six blocks visible from the back, which rules out option D. There are two blue blocks visible from the back, which rules out option B. There is one block visible on the left when viewed from the back, which rules out option C.

5.   C

Option A is ruled out because there is no four-pointed star. Option B is ruled out because the grey arrow and the grey triangle must be on opposite sides. Option D is ruled out because the heart and the three-pointed star must be on opposite sides.

6.   D

Option A is ruled out because if the black and white diamond is on the front and the grey diamond is on the top, then the black ring should be on the right. Option B is ruled out because there is no grey square. Option C is ruled out because the white cross and the black and white diamond must be on opposite sides.

7.   A

Option B is ruled out because if the triangle is on the front and the black face is on the top, then the white arrow should be on the right. Option C is ruled out because the white arrow should be pointing towards the grey arrow. Option D is ruled out because the triangle and the grey arrow must be on opposite sides.

8.   B

Option A is ruled out because the black stripe and the grey and white triangles must be on opposite sides. Option C is ruled out because the grey triangle should be closest to the circle. Option D is ruled out because the white arrow should point away from the grey and white triangles.

9.   A

Option B is ruled out because the part of the figure originally below the fold line should be visible. Options C and D are ruled out because the fold lines have moved.

10.   C

Option A is ruled out because the part of the figure originally to the left of the fold line has been rotated. Option B is ruled out because the part of the figure originally to the right of the fold line should be visible. Option D is ruled out because the part of the figure originally to the left of the fold line should be visible.

11.   A

Option B is ruled out because the part of the figure originally to the right of the fold line should be visible. Option C is ruled out because the fold line has moved. Option D is ruled out because the part of the figure originally to the right of the fold line is the wrong shape.

12.   D

Option A is ruled out because the fold line has moved. Option B is ruled out because the part of the figure that has been folded is the wrong shape. Option C is ruled out because the part of the figure originally to the left of the fold line is the wrong shape.

13.   B

Options A and C are ruled out because the part of the figure that has been folded is the wrong shape. Option D is ruled out because the fold line has moved.

14.   C

The bottom left block in C is at the back of the figure. The top block in C is in the middle of the figure. The other block is at the front.

15.   B

One of the bottom blocks in B is at the front of the figure. The other bottom block is at the back of the figure. The top block in B is arranged between them.

16.   D

The top block in D is at the back of the figure. The other two blocks are arranged in front of it.

17.   A

The top block in A is at the back of the figure. The other two blocks are arranged in front of it.

Test 27 — pages 120-123

1.   B

The third cube view is the first cube view rotated 90 degrees left-to-right. So the overlapping ovals are on the right.

2.   C

The third cube view is the first cube view rotated 90 degrees clockwise in the plane of the page, then 90 degrees away from you, top-to-bottom. So the white trapezium is on the front.

3.   A

The third cube view is the first cube view rotated 90 degrees towards you, top-to-bottom, then 180 degrees in the plane of the page. So the face with the black circle and triangles is on the top.

4.   D

The third cube view is the second cube view rotated 90 degrees clockwise in the plane of the page. So the face with the white circles joined by a line is on the front.

5. F

Shape F is rotated 90 degrees away from you, top-to-bottom.

6. D

Shape D is rotated 90 degrees anticlockwise in the plane of the page.

7. B

Shape B is rotated 90 degrees clockwise in the plane of the page. It is then rotated 90 degrees left-to-right.

8. E

Shape E is rotated 90 degrees left-to-right. It is then rotated 90 degrees towards you, top-to-bottom.

9. A

Shape A is rotated 90 degrees away from you, top-to-bottom. It is then rotated 180 degrees left-to-right.

10. C

Shape C is rotated 90 degrees left-to-right.

11. C

Options A and B are ruled out because the black ring and the grey shape are on opposite sides. Option D is ruled out because the black ring and the white shape are on opposite sides.

12. D

Option A is ruled out because the grey star on a white rectangle and the nine-pointed star are on opposite sides. Option B is ruled out because the grey star should not point towards the black lines. Option C is ruled out because if it is folded so that the nine-pointed star is on the top of the cube and the grey star on a white rectangle is at the front, then the black lines would be on the left.

13. C

Option A is ruled out because if it is folded so that the diamond is on the top and the black three-quarter circles are at the front, then the triangle would be on the left. Option B is ruled out because the triangle and the black three-quarter circles are on opposite sides. Option D is ruled out because the triangle should point towards the diamond.

14. C

Option A is ruled out because the pentagon should point towards the arrow. Option B is ruled out because the black lines and the arrow are on opposite sides. Option D is ruled out because the arrow should point towards the black lines.

15. D

There are four blocks visible from the right, which rules out options B and C. There are three rows when viewed from the right, which rules out option A.

16. B

There are seven blocks visible from the right, which rules out options C and D. The blue block is visible on the left, which rules out option A.

17. B

There are five blocks visible from the right, which rules out option C. There is only one block visible on the bottom, which rules out option A. There is a blue block visible on the left, which rules out option D.

18. B

There are six blocks visible from the right, which rules out option A. There is only one blue block visible, which rules out option D. There are three blocks visible on the top, which rules out option C.

Puzzles 9 — page 124

Witch Door?

Door C

Cube Confusion

Test 28 — pages 125-128

1. C

Option A is ruled out because the part that has been folded is too big. Option B is ruled out because the fold line has moved. Option D is ruled out because the part that has been folded is too small.

2. B

Option A is ruled out because the figure has been reflected downwards and not folded. Option C is ruled out because the part of the figure originally above the fold line is the wrong shape. Option D is ruled out because the fold line has moved.

3. A

Option B is ruled out because the shape has been rotated and then folded. Option C is ruled out because the fold line has moved. Option D is ruled out because the part of the figure originally to the left of the fold line should be visible.

4. D

Option A is ruled out because the part that has been folded is too big. Option B is ruled out because the part of the figure originally to the right of the fold line has been rotated, not folded. Option C is ruled out because the part that has been folded is the wrong shape.

5. C

Option A is ruled out because the figure has been broken apart along the fold line. Options B and D are ruled out because the part that has been folded is the wrong shape.

6. D

There should be a block two cubes long going into the page on the bottom left, which rules out options A and B. There should be a blue cube on the top left of the figure, which rules out option C.

7. A

There should be a blue cube on the top right of the figure, which rules out options B and D. There should be a block two cubes high on the left of the figure, which rules out option C.

8. B

There should be a cube at the back of the figure on the bottom left, which rules out options A and C. There should be a block two cubes long going into the page, which rules out option D.

9. C

Only one half of the two-cube-long block on the bottom right of the figure should be visible. This rules out option A. There should be a block two cubes long going into the page on the top left of the figure, which rules out options B and D.

10. C

Option A is ruled out because there is no grey heart on the net. Option B is ruled out because there is no black square on the net. Option D is ruled out because there aren't two L-shapes on the net.

11. A

Option B is ruled out because if the grey arrow shape is on the front and the white rectangle is on the side, then the black triangle should be on the right. Option C is ruled out because there is no black arrow on the net. Option D is ruled out because the curved grey shape and the grey arrow must be on opposite sides.

12. D

Option A is ruled out because if the white five-sided shape is on the front and the oval is on the right, then the grey bar-and-circles figure should be on the top. Option B is ruled out because the white five-sided shape should be pointing towards the oval. Option C is ruled out because if the black star is on the front and the white circle is on the top, then the grey bar-and-circles figure should be on the right.

13. B

Option A is ruled out because the ends of the ovals should be facing the arrowhead. Option C is ruled out because the arrowhead should be pointing towards the grey ovals. Option D is ruled out because if the ovals are on the front and the black five-sided shape is on the right, then the hexgaon should be on the top.

14. D

Option D fits on the right of the figure.

15.   B

Option B rotates 90 degrees right-to-left. It then fits on the back of the figure.

16.   C

Option C rotates 90 degrees right-to-left, then 90 degrees away from you, top-to-bottom. It then fits on the right of the figure.

17.   A

Option A rotates 90 degrees clockwise in the plane of the page. It then fits on the front of the figure.

Test 29 — pages 129-132

1.   C

There are three blocks visible from the right, which rules out options A and D. There are two blocks visible on the left-hand side, which rules out option B.

2.   B

There are five blocks visible from the right, which rules out option A. There is only one blue block visible from the right, which rules out options C and D.

3.   B

There are five blocks visible from the right, which rules out option C. There are three blocks visible in the middle column, which rules out option A. There are three blocks visible at the bottom, which rules out option D.

4.   A

There are five blocks visible from the right, which rules out option C. There are three blocks visible on the right-hand side, which rules out options B and D.

5.   D

Options A and C are ruled out because there are no grey rectangular sides on the net. Option B is ruled out because there are no white square faces on the net.

6.   B

Option A is ruled out because there is only one blue rectangular face on the net. Option C is ruled out because the triangular face should be white. Option D is ruled out because there is only one white rectangular face on the net.

7.   B

Option A is ruled out because the pentagonal face should be blue. Option C is ruled out because the pentagonal face should be white. Option D is ruled out because the top rectangular face should be blue.

8.   C

Option A is ruled out because there is only one grey rectangular side. Option B is ruled out because the pentagonal face should be grey. Option D is ruled out because the pentagonal face should be white.

9.   B

Shape B has been rotated 90 degrees towards you, top-to-bottom.

10.   C

Shape C has been rotated 90 degrees right-to-left.

11.   F

Shape F has been rotated 180 degrees right-to-left.

12.   A

Shape A has been rotated 90 degrees towards you, top-to-bottom. It has then been rotated 90 degrees anticlockwise in the plane of the page.

13.   D

Shape D has been rotated 90 degrees towards you, top-to-bottom. It has then been rotated 180 degrees in the plane of the page.

14.   E

Shape E has been rotated 180 degrees right-to-left. It has then been rotated 90 degrees towards you, top-to-bottom.

15.   D

The top right block in D is at the back right of the figure. The other two blocks are arranged to its left.

16.   B

The bottom block in B is at the front of the figure. The other two blocks are arranged above and behind it.

17.   A

The top block in A is on the left of the figure. The other two blocks are arranged to the right of it.

18.   A

The top left block in A is at the back of the figure. The other two blocks are arranged in front of it.

Test 30 — pages 133-136

1.   D

There are four blocks visible from the top, which rules out options A and C. There is one block visible on the left when viewed from the top, which rules out option B.

2.   B

There are seven blocks visible from the top, which rules out options C and D. There are three blocks visible on the left when viewed from the top, which rules out option A.

3.   A

There are six blocks visible from the top, which rules out option B. There are two blocks visible on the right when viewed from the top, which rules out option C. There are two blocks visible on the left when viewed from the top, which rules out option D.

4.   B

There are two blocks visible on the right when viewed from the top, which rules out options A and C. There is only one blue block visible when viewed from the top, which rules out option D.

5.   C

Option A is ruled out because the fold line is in the wrong place. Option B is ruled out because the part that has been folded is the wrong shape. Option D is ruled out because the part that has been folded has been reflected.

6.   B

Option A is ruled out because the part of the figure originally above the fold line should be visible. Option C is ruled out because the part that has been folded is the wrong shape. Option D is ruled out because the fold line is in the wrong place.

7.   D

Options A and C are ruled out because the part that has been folded is the wrong shape. Option B is ruled out because the part of the figure originally to the right of the fold line should be visible.

8.   C

Option A is ruled out because the fold line is in the wrong place. Option B is ruled out because the part that has been folded is too small. Option D is ruled out because the fold line has been rotated.

9.   A

Options B and C are ruled out because the part that has been folded is the wrong shape. Option D is ruled out because the part that has been folded has been rotated.

10.   A

Options B and C are ruled out because the grey triangle and the black circles are on opposite sides. Option D is ruled out because the grey triangle and the white cross are on opposite sides.

11.   B

Option A is ruled out because the black arrow should point towards the white diamond. Option C is ruled out because the black arrow and the white circles are on opposite sides. Option D is ruled out because the black arrow and the white diamond are on opposite sides.

12.   D

Option A is ruled out because the grey triangle and the white star are on opposite sides. Option B is ruled out because if it is folded so that the white star is on the top of the cube and the grey triangle is on the right, then the black stripes would be at the back. Option C is ruled out because the black stripes should not touch the face with the grey triangle.

13. C

Option A is ruled out because if it is folded so that the grey arrow is on the front of the cube and the black drop is on the top, then the white circle would be on the left. Option B is ruled out because the grey arrow and the white circle are on opposite sides. Option D is ruled out because the grey arrow should point towards the circle.

14. A

There should be one cube, which rules out options B and C. There should be a cube closest when viewed from above, which rules out option D.

15. D

There should be two blocks in the closest layer when viewed from above, which rules out options A and C. One of these should be a cube, which rules out option B.

16. C

There should be a cube in front of a block three cubes long (or blocks equivalent to this) on the right-hand side, which rules out options A and B. There should be a block two cubes tall in the centre, which rules out option D.

17. A

There should be a block two cubes long lying on its side at the left-hand side of the figure. This rules out options C and D. There should not be a block on top of this, which rules out option B.

Test 31 — pages 137-140

1. A

Shape A is rotated 90 degrees away from you, top-to-bottom.

2. F

Shape F is rotated 90 degrees right-to-left.

3. D

Shape D is rotated 90 degrees towards you, top-to-bottom. It is then rotated 90 degrees clockwise in the plane of the page.

4. B

Shape B is rotated 90 degrees right-to-left. It is then rotated 180 degrees towards you, top-to-bottom.

5. B

There are five blocks visible from above, which rules out options A and D. There are three blocks visible on the right-hand side, which rules out option C.

6. D

There are five blocks visible from above, which rules out option B. There is only one blue block visible from above, which rules out option C. There are two blocks visible on the left-hand side, which rules out option A.

7. A

There are five blocks visible from above, which rules out option B. There are two blocks visible at the front, which rules out options C and D.

8. D

There are six blocks visible from above, which rules out option B. There are two blocks visible at the back, which rules out option C. There is only one block visible on the left-hand side, which rules out option A.

9. C

Option A is ruled out because the circle and the hexagon must be on opposite sides. Option B is ruled out because there is no white cross on the net. Option D is ruled out because the diamond and the cross must be on opposite sides.

10. C

Option A is ruled out because there are not two black crosses on the net. Options B and D are ruled out because the black and grey lines and the white star must be on opposite sides.

11. A

Option B is ruled out because the white line in the circle should point towards the kite. Option C is ruled out because the pentagon and the star must be on opposite sides. Option D is ruled out because one of the grey triangles should be next to the star.

12. A

Option B is ruled out because the side with two black circles has the wrong rotation. Option C is ruled out because if the grey circle is on the front and the white rectangles are on top, then the black and white square should be on the left. Option D is ruled out because the hexagons have the wrong rotation.

13. B

Option A is ruled out because the figure has been broken apart along the fold line. Option C is ruled out because the part of the figure that has been folded is the wrong shape. Option D is ruled out because the fold line has moved.

14. D

Option A is ruled out because the part of the figure that has been folded is the wrong shape. Option B is ruled out because the part of the figure originally below the fold line should still be visible. Option C is ruled out because the figure has been broken apart along the fold line.

15. B

Option A is ruled out because the part of the figure that has been folded is the wrong shape. Option C is ruled out because the part of the figure that has not been folded is the wrong shape. Option D is ruled out because the part of the figure originally to the right of the fold line should still be visible.

16. A

Option B is ruled out because the fold line has moved. Option C is ruled out because the part of the figure originally below the fold line should still be visible. Option D is ruled out because the part of the figure originally above the fold line has been rotated, not folded.

17. D

Option A is ruled out because the fold line has moved. Options B and C are ruled out because the part of the figure that has not been folded is the wrong shape.

Puzzles 10 — page 141

Geometric Gerald
Nets C and D